bumpy
rides
and soft
landings

Stories of Coming Out,
Flying High, and
Not Learning to
Play the Piano

James Pauley, Jr.

TAKE FLIGHT PUBLISHING, LLC

Published by Take Flight Publishing, LLC
www.jpauleyauthor.com

ISBN (hardcover): 979-8-9867516-0-3
ISBN (paperback): 979-8-9867516-1-0
ISBN (e-book): 979-8-9867516-2-7

Quoted material used in the book comes from the following sources:
Arthur Richardson and Ross MacLean, "Too Fat Polka," recorded August 1947, Shapiro, Bernstein & Co. Inc., released 29 September 1947.
Jaromir Vejvoda, composer, "Beer Barrel Polka," lyrics by Lew Brown and Wladimir A. Timm, published 1939, Shapiro, Bernstein & Co. Inc.

Book design and production by Domini Dragoone, www.dominidragoone.com
Edited by Jennifer Huston Schaeffer, www.whitedogeditorial.com
Cover photos: Courtesy of the author, Domini Dragoone, and iStock.com

For Rich,
my soulmate and best friend.

Your love and support sustain
me each and every day.

Contents

Preface vii

Next Generations 1

Hoot and Holler 11

Try as They May 33

Bitten by the Bug 59

Come Out, Come Out 85

A Smile or a Smirk? 105

In Tune 113

Mean Old Queen 133

Lest Ye Judge 149

Pea Ewe 157

A Cure for Crusty......................... 169

A New Attitude 189

Prisoners to a Cell........................ 203

In Stitches 213

Love Always.............................. 223

So Sari................................... 245

Laugh That One Off....................... 263

PITA..................................... 273

Epilogue 283

Acknowledgments.......................... 285

About the Author 287

Preface

I was born in 1956 and brought up in the small town of Edwardsburg, Michigan. Although the village had a relatively low population, it was large in area due to the vast farmland and many lakes. It was a great place to grow up, where everyone knew almost everyone else.

My parents were married at the young age of eighteen and over the next nine years had my sister, me, and my brother. As the middle child, I was stereotypical in many ways: fiercely independent, a peacemaker, a trustworthy friend, and a seeker of fairness and justice. My parents divorced when I was six, and my peacemaking and fairness-seeking traits went into major overdrive. I wanted them back together so they could be like all the other parents: married, even if they were miserable. But it wasn't meant to be.

Although my childhood was anything but conventional, I have wonderful memories of fun times, a lot of love and laughter, delicious home-cooked meals every day, and quality time spent with each of my parents. And even though as a child I wasn't happy with the situation, I'm now very thankful because it helped make me what I am today: eclectic, loving, diverse, tenacious, and open-minded.

As a youngster, I was a brat and drove my poor mother crazy. In retrospect, I was probably acting out the anger and frustration I was feeling at the time. I can still be a brat at times, and for the past forty years, I've been driving my spouse, Rich, crazy. It's no longer out of anger and frustration, though; it's just fun.

I was always a good student, but I had to work hard and study a lot. It didn't come easy, but it certainly paid off. In 1978, I fulfilled one of my biggest dreams by becoming a flight attendant. For the next thirty-five years, I worked for a large commercial airline, jet-setting all over the world. Soon after retiring from that, I found another flight attendant gig, this time with a private airline. While in training for the latter, I found out quickly that I had to deprogram myself of all things commercial and learn a new set of skills for the private sector. It was a completely different world. I also had to sign a confidentiality agreement because we fly some very well-known people all over the planet. That was a tough one for me, though, because . . . well . . . I like to share things. And some of the things I've heard and seen on those little jets are just *begging* to be shared.

But I can't. So for now, I'll just have to stick to the things I *am* allowed to tell.

Next
Generations

I'm a person of simple means because I come from a family of simple means. They're the salt of the earth, one might say, my father's side especially. My dad's relatives hail from West (by God) Virginia. And no, I'm not talking about Morgantown, Wheeling, or some of those other highfalutin places. I'm talking about the tiny coal mining towns set so far back in the hills and hollows you'd need a search party to find them.

"Our own little bit of heaven," my father's family used to say. "Now don't be tellin' nobody 'cause it's all we got."

My father's life has not always been easy. His father was a hard-drinking and stubborn womanizer. My father's mother was an angel. They met when she was an old maid of fifteen. Having just finished his shift in the coal mines of West Virginia, he emerged blackened and exhausted after spending the day in the bowels of the earth. My grandmother didn't even know what he looked like until the following Saturday or, as they called it, Bath Day. A romance ensued, and with the help of a shotgun barrel rammed halfway up his rear, my grandfather asked my grandmother to be his wife. His *pregnant* wife, that is. Many years later, my sister, Deb, and I very craftily and somewhat sneakily coerced our sweet grandmother into giving us more specific dates and details. We walked away in absolute shock. Our saintly grandmother—a good Christian woman—had been knocked up when she got married. However, she miscarried that pregnancy, so she didn't actually become a mother until she gave birth to a baby boy at the ripe old age of seventeen.

Two more children—both boys—quickly followed. Fatherhood didn't have much of an effect on my grandfather. Although he never missed work, a lot of his money was spent on drinking and carousing in the neighboring towns. He was known for his quick temper and often instigated bar fights. When I was a child, I once asked him how he got the scar on his neck.

"Oh, some ole bastard stabbed me back in nineteen and thirty six. I 'bout bled to death," he chuckled as he took a long drag from his hand-rolled cigarette.

Not surprisingly, my grandmother served as both parents to her sons for many years. She was a nurturing, loving mother who made their clothes, raised a garden every year to feed them, and helped teach them to read over a kerosene lantern. She also instilled in each of them an incredible work ethic.

Until he was sixteen, my father lived with his family in a quiet hollow tucked between two lush, green mountains. Fumbach Hollow (pronounced Fum-Buck by the locals) was a peaceful haven with perhaps forty lifelong residents. A babbling brook made its twisting journey down the side of Coaldale Mountain, the larger of the two. The brook eventually found solace at the bottom of the mountain, where it slowed and widened as it continued its merry way over much flatter, yet rocky, terrain. Once it reached this point, it was relatively level and shallow, so parts of it also served as the only road leading into "Fumbuck Holler."

In the early 1900s, a Mr. Fumbach discovered the hollow that was later named for him. His first name was always the topic of much debate. Many claimed it was Nipper; others argued it was Heinrich, stating that Nipper was the horse Mr. Fumbach was riding when he entered the hollow for the first time. But the naysayers—no pun intended—insisted that Heinrich was the horse.

By the time my grandpa decided they were moving to Indiana in the early 1950s, my grandmother was probably more than ready to leave her life of hardship. And besides, for the first time in her life, she would have electricity and running water.

Grandpa, who'd never worked anywhere except the coal mines, took a factory job shortly after arriving in Elkhart, a town in northern Indiana, about half an hour east of South Bend. Around that time, he was diagnosed with rheumatoid arthritis, but he still never missed a day of work. His drinking continued after the move, but he saved it mostly for the weekends.

Even though life was decidedly better for her in Indiana, my grandma soon escaped Grandpa's taunting and ridicule by joining a church and diving in headfirst. Sister Pauley became a fixture of the church, never missing a service, prayer meeting, or retreat.

My own parents married just three days after my mother's eighteenth birthday. Dad was just a few months older. Three kids and nine years later, they divorced. My father moved in with his parents, so my sister and I started spending every weekend with them. My little brother, Scott, was still a baby, so he stayed home with our mother.

The scenario was nearly the same every Saturday. Dad would pick us up at noon and then, depending on the time of year, we'd go bowling, swimming, miniature golfing, or to watch him pitch horseshoes. The latter wasn't my favorite, especially since I still had a pretty clear recollection of when Judy Everton, the extremely nearsighted teenage girl next door mistook little Jimmy for a horseshoe peg. Eight stitches and two years later, I still couldn't quite shake that memory, but I'd learned to use it to my advantage.

"Hey, Dad, remember that time you and Judy Everton were pitching horseshoes, and she hit me right above the eye?" I would ask. Then, trying to look as pitiful as possible, I'd practically whisper, "It still hurts sometimes."

Guilt worked like a charm with my father.

"Uh, yeah, I remember," he'd say, jiggling the change in his pocket as he looked down at his feet. Suddenly, he'd brighten up and say, "Why don't we run over to that variety store next to the barber shop. Maybe you kids would like a game or something."

We didn't want a game; we wanted the "or something." Deb and I usually chose candy—lots and *lots* of candy—or some sort of craft project, which was not what typical boys my age would've chosen. But, then again, I wasn't a typical boy.

"Now don't overdo it with the candy," Dad would caution.

"Ooh, my eye," I'd whine, rubbing the almost-invisible scar. Then Deb and I would leave with anything our conniving little hearts desired.

I vividly remember the summer when I was eight. With horseshoe season in full swing, so to speak, and the Elkhart County 4-H Fair fast approaching, Dad was determined to win the horseshoe-pitching contest at the fair. So he started practicing every day, Saturdays and Sundays included.

That meant Deb and I would sit for hours at the edge of the horseshoe courts. We'd busy ourselves with various projects, all the while munching on candy. We used a loom to create chocolate-stained pot holders by the hundreds. We cranked out one paint by numbers masterpiece after another with brushes stuck to our taffy-laden fingers. We even took a liking to mosaics, making everything from ashtrays to plates to boxes big enough to house a pound of jelly beans. We also learned to knit dishcloths, balancing knitting needles and licorice in our hands at the same time. Knit one, purl two, bite. Knit one, purl two, bite. It was an absolute miracle that I never broke a tooth by accidentally biting into the knitting needle instead of the licorice.

Looking back, we must've been a huge embarrassment to our sports-loving father, but he never showed it. In fact, he always brought his friends over to the sidelines to introduce them to his chubby children.

Dad took first place in the horseshoe-throwing contest at the fair that year, winning yet another trophy to add to his already impressive collection. That fall, after horseshoe season ended, we moved our ever-increasing talents to Grandma Pauley's kitchen table. In September, I got my own wood-burning kit for my birthday and was soon branding everything in sight. For her birthday in November, Deb got a portable sewing machine and began sewing stretch panels into our rapidly shrinking clothes. We were becoming creative geniuses, not only in the artistic sense but also in the lying to our grandmother sense.

We loved going to the movies, but Sister Pauley's religion forbade it. "Jimmy, movies are the work of the devil himself," she would say. "You don't wanna be part of that evil by goin' to one of them dirty ole thee-ay-ters, now do ya? Why, I've heard people just sit there kissin' and a-carryin' on, just like the ole devil wants. No sir, you ain't goin' to no movies. I recollect hearin' a story from Sister Morgan about her grandson who used to go to them ole movies. He's in reform school now, where he belongs. Bless his heart . . . his evil heart from all them movies."

Alright, already, I thought. But that didn't stop us from asking our father. "Dad," Deb or I would whisper, "*James Bond 007* is playing at the Elco."

That's all it took, knowing what a huge fan he was. "You know, people are always telling me I look just like Sean Connery," Dad would say.

"Well, you *do*," we'd fib, knowing it would get us a little closer to what we wanted: the movie and Sweet Tarts.

Dad didn't have a problem taking us, but even he was fearful of the repercussions should Grandma find out. Plus, we could never look in the paper for showtimes because Grandma was always watching us like a hawk.

I was a teenager before I realized you were actually supposed to enter a theater before the movie started. When I was a child, we'd simply walk in whenever we could make a break from Grandma. Often, we'd arrive at the theater just in time to see James Bond driving his Ferrari in a high-speed chase or him in a heart-shaped bed with Honor Blackman, who was trying to suck the tonsils right out of his throat. It kind of took something out of watching the beginning when you'd already seen the ending. But that was okay because we'd return full of buttered popcorn and Sweet Tarts, just in time to sit down for Grandma Pauley's homemade beef and noodles, fried chicken, mashed potatoes and gravy, green beans and bacon, coleslaw, corn on the cob, tomatoes, and buttermilk biscuits. And just like the movie, we knew what the grand finale would be—her mouthwatering banana pudding.

Saturday nights were always the same at Grandma and Grandpa Pauley's house. There was never any deviation. Dad would leave around seven o'clock for his night on the town. He had a reputation to uphold, looking like Sean Connery and all. Besides, he was a real hit with the ladies.

In the meantime, Deb and I would sit in the living room with our grandparents. By the mid-1960s, they'd only recently purchased their first television, a rather large (for the era) color console that Deb and I weren't even allowed to touch. At precisely seven o'clock, we'd find ourselves planted in front of the TV watching *The King Family Show*, a variety show featuring the multi-talented King Sisters and about seventy-three of their family members. This was a great way to ease into the *real* entertainment for the evening: *The Lawrence Welk Show*, which lasted one agonizingly long and painful hour, interrupted only twice by our friends at Brylcreem. And what a welcomed interruption it was. "A little dab'll do ya!" meant that for two minutes, we didn't have to listen to the Lennon Sisters.

As the weeks progressed, I longed for *Get Smart* and *Gilligan's*

Island. Just a simple turn of the channel knob, and we would be home free. But my grandparents wouldn't dream of it.

Although Deb and I delighted in fighting with one another, we shared a mutual desire to watch *anything* but Lawrence Welk. Or so I thought. One night, as we sat watching Bobby and Barbara wiggling across the dance floor doing the mambo, I couldn't help but notice that Bobby's pants were tighter than usual. Suddenly, a movement to the right caught my attention. As I turned to see what it was, I was horrified to see my sister's foot tapping to the beat. *Uh-oh . . . I've lost her,* I thought. *Now who am I going to fight with?* With sadness in my eyes, I returned my gaze to Bobby's pants.

The following Sunday was cold and rainy, and the only movies showing were *Mary Poppins* and *The Absent-minded Professor,* which we'd already seen, so Dad suggested we go meet his new lady friend. He must've picked up on our disinterest because he sweetened the pot, saying, "You can have all the french fries you want."

Sold! We were soon on our way to Cobert Lake Bar and Grill.

The place was hopping. Literally. People young and old crowded the dance floor, and the common denominator they shared soon became apparent: they *loved* to polka. And eat. And drink. And sing.

"I don't want her, you can have her, she's too fat for me!" bellowed the singer, rattling the smoke-covered windows.

When Dad spotted his lady friend, who had obviously been there for a while, he threw us a couple of bills and said, "Go ahead and get your fries. And order me a beer." Then he and his lady friend polkaed off to the dance floor, hand in hand.

As we sat there, eating french fry after french fry, Deb and I realized that the music was becoming more and more infectious. We couldn't believe it! As our feet began thumping on the sticky floor, old ladies with blue hair teased almost as high as the ceiling fans laughed as they glided arm in arm around the dance floor. Other ancient codgers, no doubt taking a brief hiatus from their oxygen tanks, floated by as they wheezed sweet nothings into the hearing aids of their female dance partners.

Deb and I couldn't get to the dance floor fast enough. All the weeks of watching Bobby and Barbara were about to pay off. Maybe *The Lawrence Welk Show* wasn't so bad after all. Maybe it was actually a blessing in disguise.

Despite the fun I was having, something started eating at me. If my grandma didn't think it was befitting for us to even be in a movie theater, how would she feel about us being in a liquor-infested, dance-provoking, foul-mouthed atmosphere of fun? Would she ever forgive me? *God, why couldn't she be Polish?*

When we returned to the table, Dad downed another beer and Deb and I downed another order of french fries. Then we started arguing about who got the longer fry. But as soon as the band returned from a much-needed break and the music started, we stopped our bickering midsentence, grabbed each other's hand, and skidded onto the dance floor.

"Roll out the barrel, we'll have a beer barrel of fun . . ."

Hoot and
Holler

Every summer after my parents divorced, my father would load Deb and me into his 1960 Chevy Biscayne for our yearly trek to his boyhood home. Our brother, Scott, had severe asthma, so he always stayed at home with our mother.

My memories from those trips are, at times, a bit hazy. Time has erased many of the finer details, and those that remain have melded together, but one that comes to mind was from July of 1966. Why that one stands out more than the rest, I really don't know. Maybe it was because I was a very impressionable boy of nine who was still trying desperately to understand how his tidy little family unit had been severed a few years earlier. In my young mind, my parents' divorce seemed so unnecessary. More than anything, I wanted to repair the damage and get my parents back together so we could resume our lives and enjoy a blissful existence, just like on *The Donna Reed Show.*

Although I feigned excitement to be going to West Virginia, the reality was that I didn't want to leave my mother. I worried about her being home alone with my younger brother and her new boyfriend. I just knew she was going to be *so* lonely.

But when I hinted that I didn't want to go, she screamed, "By God, you are *going* with your father! It says in the divorce settlement that your father gets you kids for one week every summer. And you're not getting out of it, young man!"

Is this actually a cry for help? I wondered. *Maybe she's really trying to say, "Please, oh PLEASE, don't leave me!"*

But I knew I had to go. There was a family reunion, and people were coming from all over the world—or at least from Indiana and some neighboring hollows.

When the day of the trip arrived, we loaded up the Biscayne. My grandparents were riding with us, so my grandmother had made snacks for the long journey. Actually, she packed enough food to last several weeks, just in case we got stranded or lost. My grandfather had planned accordingly too, finding various places to stash his gin bottles should we encounter any dry counties en route. Always thinking ahead those two.

We left in the evening, after my father had already worked a full day at his factory job. My sister and I passed the hours doing something much more constructive than sleeping: bickering . . . nonstop . . . for ten hours. Despite the expletives my father used repeatedly, Deb and me arguing was actually a blessing in disguise. Not only did it help keep my weary father awake on the overnight journey, it also redirected my focus and my concern for my mother.

As we pulled into Fumbuck Holler at six the next morning and our father maneuvered the car down the narrow road, Deb and I quickly quieted down. Although the road/brook was shallow at this point, I worried that with one wrong turn of the steering wheel, we'd all be washed away, never to be seen again. But about two hundred yards into the hollow, my father steered the car sharply to the left then stopped at the base of a steep mountain.

"Do we have to get out and climb that thing?" I asked.

Without answering, my father ground the gears of the Biscayne until he finally found first, then he revved up the tired engine. As we lurched forward practically at a ninety-degree angle, I wondered how we were going to make it to the top without tipping backward.

"Ain't it good to be back home?" my grandmother announced loudly over the sound of overworked pistons and crunching gravel.

"Our little bit of heaven," my grandfather slurred as he tried to focus on the pint of gin in his hand.

The car continued its ascent for a few more minutes before suddenly leveling off. We'd reached the top of the mountain. In front of us lay a large, flat parcel of land with a big white clapboard house and a dilapidated barn that obviously hadn't seen a paintbrush for a decade—or ten.

A few yards to the right of the barn was a huge verdant garden, home to an array of vegetables and fruit: zucchini, peppers, tomatoes, green beans, okra, lettuce, carrots, corn, cantaloupe, and watermelon. A sloping fence lazily surrounded the garden, guarding it haphazardly from the livestock that seemed to be everywhere.

At least two dozen chickens clucked annoyingly as they tried in vain to outrun an old, yet frisky, rooster. They crisscrossed the driveway in front of us, oblivious that their Yankee kin had arrived. As I glanced out the car window, I noticed a cow standing near the side of the barn. She slowly lifted her head at the unfamiliar sound of a motorized vehicle, then she eyed us quizzically for a moment before letting her head drop back down to her much more interesting task of plucking and chewing the long grass that tickled her bulging udders. Pigs grunted and squealed gleefully as they inhaled their breakfast in the barnyard. And as we came to a stop, a flea-ridden hound mustered up every bit of strength he had left to let out a barely audible *Woof!* Barn cats stepped over him in the quest for some tasty hillbilly mice.

An ancient brown mare swished her tail and whinnied, just as a billy goat discovered a pair of sun-dried underpants hanging on the clothesline.

"Who lives here again?" I questioned.

My grandmother was the first to answer. "This here's where my sister Hootie lives. This is where she raised all them young'uns."

"How many . . . uh . . . young'uns does she have?" I asked, looking around.

"Lord, how many does she have, Willy?" she asked my grandfather, who had suddenly decided to take a nap.

"I believe she got fifteen," Grandma continued, answering her own question. "Plus, she raised the two Homer Joe had when she married him. So that makes . . . let's see now . . . fifteen, sixteen, seventeen in all. I hear she's mindin' two of the grandbabies now too."

A real-life version of *Ma and Pa Kettle Back on the Farm* was unfolding right before my eyes. "What's Hootie short for?" I wondered out loud.

"Hoot, I guess," my father answered, as he set the parking brake. "Is that right, Mom?"

"It's Hootany, I reckon."

"Hootany? Is that like *hootenanny?*" my sister giggled. "Did they run out of names by the time they got to her?"

"Nah, she's the firstborn. And I think you been watchin' too much of *The Beverly Hillbillies*, young lady."

How I loved seeing my sister make a fool of herself.

Just then, the back door of the house burst open and a woman and a slew of children came running to greet us. "Lord, have mercy. Gladie, is that you? My baby sister's done come home again!" Aunt Hootie embraced my grandmother before hesitantly reaching for my grandfather, who was just opening his eyes and undoubtedly wondering where the hell he was.

"And Willy, nice to see you too."

After the commotion died down, we followed Aunt Hootie into the house where she led us to our room. Not rooms . . . just one room. Granted, it was a large bedroom, but it appeared smaller because it contained three double beds. Although it was cramped, it had a light and airy feel to it, due in part to the bright sunlight shining through the pair of floor-to-ceiling windows on the far wall. On each bed lay a colorful, hand-stitched quilt. Later, my grandmother told me that Aunt Hootie had made a quilt during each of her pregnancies, which equates to a shitload of quilts. Had she had any more kids, she might've put the Amish out of business.

The room was immaculate. And I don't just mean it was clean; it was absolutely spotless. Crocheted doilies adorned the antique dresser and nightstands, on top of which stood vases with freshly cut snapdragons, zinnias, and roses. I was impressed. Deb and I quickly chose the beds we'd be sharing, me and my father in one, my sister and grandmother in another, and my grandfather and his gin bottles in the other.

Clang! Clang! Clang!

"BREAKFAST!" Aunt Hootie shouted. "Y'all come and eat now, ya hear!"

That was music to my ears because I was starving after the long trip. The music was short-lived, however, when a new sound threatened to shatter my eardrums.

Not more than half an hour earlier, when we'd first arrived, I had witnessed every type of animal imaginable: a cow, a horse, a mangy dog, cats, chickens, a horny rooster, pigs, and a goat. What I didn't recall seeing was a herd of elephants— which now appeared to be noisily descending the stairs. The elephants quickly made their way toward three picnic tables that were lined up end to end from the front entry all the way down the hallway to the kitchen. Enough vittles were scattered across the picnic tables to feed an entire army—or, in this case, my family.

Then I saw, or rather heard, the baby elephant. "Granny, where the *hell* is my breakfast!" boomed a voice, which appeared to be that of a child.

As the room fell silent, I saw my grandmother wince before closing her eyes in prayer. I was quite certain she was asking for forgiveness that someone, especially someone so young, had just used the word *hell* in a sentence other than a Bible verse.

My eyes turned to find the source of this foul language. Filling the lower half of the doorway was perhaps the shortest, widest child I had ever seen.

"Donny Boy, you simmer down now, ya hear," Aunt Hootie said to her four-year-old grandson in a stern, yet loving, way. "We's got company. Lookie here now, your Aunt Gladie came all the way from Indiana."

"I said, I's hungry!" Donny Boy growled as he stomped his foot with such force that dishes and pans rattled in the cupboards.

Suddenly, Uncle Homer Joe appeared out of nowhere and said, "Don't make me take a switch to you, boy."

Aunt Hootie quickly dished up a plate for her four-year-old grandson. It easily could've fed a Yankee family of five, livestock included. Watching as biscuits, gravy, eggs, grits, ham, fried potatoes, tomatoes, bacon, and fresh cantaloupe were heaped on young Donny Boy's plate, I wondered if there'd be any food left for us.

With Donny Boy's mouth full for the next several minutes, the rest of us were able to visit with one another. It was short-lived, though, because Donny Boy was a fast eater. "I wanna ride my bike—*NOW!*" he screamed as pieces of food shot out of his mouth, like pellets from a BB gun.

"Now, honey, you hush up. We's tryin' to talk," Aunt Hootie said calmly. "You go out on the front porch and ride that ole bike now, ya hear."

With great effort and a lot of grunting, Donny Boy scooted off the picnic bench and lumbered to the front door. In all my nine years, I'd never seen a four-year-old lumber before.

A bit of normalcy returned momentarily, but then all of a sudden we heard, *CLUNK, CLUNK, CLUNK* followed by a child's giggling.

"Donny Boy, I don't want you ridin' that ole bike down them stairs now, ya hear."

"I ain't ridin' it down no stairs, Granny."

"Okay, honey."

CLUNK, CLUNK, CLUNK!

"Donald. Did you hear me?"

17

"Yes ma'am."

CLUNK, CLUNK, CLUNK!

"Now dammit, you little sombitch!" Uncle Homer Joe bellowed as he jumped off his bench. "Your granny said to stop it, and y'all had better stop it before I give you a lickin'!"

We heard one more *clunk* followed by heavy, frantic footsteps. Then the front door flew open, and a green-faced child sporting four green chins raced down the hallway. "Oh, Granny, I'm gonna . . . *burp* . . . I think I'm gonna . . . *burp* . . . gonna be . . . *BLECK* . . ."

Just then, the remains of Donny Boy's breakfast spurted through the air before raining down on all three picnic tables and their occupants. Those with weaker stomachs upchucked as well while the rest of us ran out the front door.

A few minutes later, after standing on the front porch shell-shocked, Clara, one of Aunt Hootie's daughters, turned to her sisters and said, "Well, c'mon girls, we best clean up."

"I'll help too," I chimed in since, at home, one of my daily chores was to help with the dishes. Otherwise, I didn't get my twenty-five-cent weekly allowance.

"Why, Lord, you silly boy, that's a girl's job," Clara laughed.

"Oh, okay." I smiled, thankfully, as I realized the joke was really on them.

As Clara picked up a large bucket, I politely asked, "Excuse me, where's your bathroom?"

"My *what*?" She seemed confused.

"Uh, your toilet. I have to . . . you know . . . I gotta go."

"Oh, you mean the crapper! It's up yonder behind the barn. I'm goin' up there to fetch some water for the dishes. Follow me."

As we made our way up to the crapper, it dawned on me

that my family must be the upper crust of Fumbuck Holler. Not only was their outhouse built directly over the rapidly descending brook, it was also at the highest point of the holler. In other words, they were the "givers," not the "receivers." And as the wooden structure stood there proudly, you could almost hear it boast, "I'm a two-seater!"

Entering for the first time, I quickly spotted a stack of catalogs, no doubt placed there for our reading pleasure. They sat right between the two "butt holes," a term my grandmother found very disturbing. Two small, extremely sturdy wooden boxes, one slightly taller than the other, stood in front of one of the holes. I figured they were makeshift stairs for the shorter members of the clan. I didn't need them, so I chose the other hole. As I carefully sat down to avoid possible splinters, I peered through the glassless window and was awestruck by the view of the hollow below. It was absolutely breathtaking. And so was the smell when Donny Boy decided to join me a few minutes later.

Without even a courtesy knock, the door flew open. I had to squint in the morning sunlight to identify my visitor, who happened to fill the lower half of the door frame. He hurriedly made his way to the vacant butt hole, climbed the makeshift stairs, and plopped down next to me.

I picked up a catalog and pretended to read.

Through clenched teeth, Donny Boy started a chant of sorts. "Shit, shit, I's got to shit. Shit, shit, I's got to shit."

I worried that my grandmother might be within hearing range and would wash both of our mouths out with soap. Finally, after one last "I's got to *shiiiit!*" he let out a long grunt, stiffened, then slumped down and sat there panting. I looked out the window in time to see a log as big around as a mountain ash tree making its way downstream.

Although I hadn't finished my own job, I decided it was time to make my exit. Call me "poop-shy," but I just wasn't comfortable having a guest during what had always been a somewhat private time for me. Plus, I worried that if I sat there too long, some muskrat, coon, or mean-spirited trout would jump up and bite me in the butt.

By the second day, I was starting to acclimate. I kept telling myself this wasn't a whole lot different than camping with my Cub Scout troop. Truth be told, though, I was homesick. Not only did I miss my mother terribly, I also longed for the luxuries I'd once taken for granted, like flushing toilets and television.

As we sat down to breakfast on that second morning, I found myself sharing the picnic bench with Buster, Aunt Hootie's oldest son, and I remembered my grandmother's warning: "You'd best stay away from Buster. He ain't quite right in the head. Had a real high fever when he was just a young'un. And do you know he's never been more than twenty miles from home?"

Just then, Buster looked down at me and smiled broadly, making me realize that the nearest dentist must've been at least twenty-one miles away. "Hey, Jimmy, after breakfast I want to show you somethin'."

"Okay," I said. I couldn't take my eyes off his single tooth. I vowed right then and there to brush my teeth regularly after every meal.

We finished our breakfast, and as the girls began clearing the table, Buster jumped up and said, "Come on, Jimmy!"

I followed him down the hallway, and as he pulled me into the living room, he exclaimed, "Lookie here! I bet you ain't never seen so many comic books before!"

I hadn't. For as far as the eye could possibly see in the long, narrow room, the walls were adorned—no *covered*—with comics, including *Beetle Bailey*, *Little Lulu*, *Archie*, *Richie Rich,* and *Nancy*. Buster had meticulously ripped out the pages and pasted them onto every square inch of wall space. Even the doors were covered! It was the most practical wallpaper I'd ever seen.

"And you know what?" Buster beamed with pride. "I've done read 'em all. Did you know I could read?"

"Wow, this is really neat, Buster." I could hardly contain my excitement.

As his face reddened from the compliment, he bit his bottom lip with his lone upper tooth. "Oh gosh, Jimmy, it's just an ole hobby of mine. Comic books is everythin' to me. That and my hound dog, Buster Junior."

Just then, as if on cue, the old dog limped into the room. It was the first time I'd seen him up close. He made his way to a ratty, hand-loomed rug next to the wood stove and, with great effort, dropped to the floor. He snapped at some invisible bugs, then launched into a determined, yet futile, attempt to rid himself of a colony or two of the hundreds of fleas who'd taken up residence in his mangy fur. As he snapped at the air around his head, I saw that he didn't have many teeth either. With his balding head and almost toothless grin, he actually sort of resembled his namesake.

"How old is your . . . uh . . . hound dog, Buster?"

"Oh Lord, I reckon he must be fifteen or sixteen now. This girl I used to know gave him to me," Buster Senior replied as he gazed longingly out the window. "Round 'bout fifteen or sixteen years ago, I believe, I met this here girl who had just moved down yonder." He pointed his long-nailed finger toward the window.

"Ever'one said she'd got hit with the ugly stick, but you know what, Jimmy? She was 'bout the purtiest thing I ever did see. We started goin' for walks together, then before I knowed it, we was goin' to church together and such."

He smiled at me . . . a smile filled with sadness—and one tooth. "One day, she brung me this here li'l pup. Found him up the mountain, all alone just a-yelpin' and a-carryin' on. His mama must've left him there to die."

He reached down and rubbed Buster Junior's scabby ears. "Well, I took one look at him, and I knowed what I had to do. He been here ever since."

"What happened to the girl?" I asked.

Buster looked at me, surprised by my curiosity. "Well, she and her family left the holler a few years back." His words trailed off and he paused a moment before continuing, "But ya know what, Jimmy?" he said, sounding more upbeat. "I still have my ole hound dog."

We both looked down at the loudly snoring dog. Suddenly, he sat bolt upright, realizing he had forgotten a very important part of self-grooming. As he tended to it, Aunt Hootie strolled into the room and grumbled, "Good Lord, Buster. Quit lickin' your crotch. You keep that up and your last good tooth is gonna rot right outta your head."

Buster Senior cackled as he said, "Why Mama, I ain't a-lickin' my crotch. I can't even get down that far. Besides, I was just tellin' Jimmy how I got this ole hound dog."

Buster Junior grunted and hoisted himself to a standing position. Then he lifted his nose and started sniffing in my direction. As his cloudy eyes focused on me, he wagged his scraggly tail and started moving toward me.

"Look Jimmy, I think that ole dog likes you!" clapped Aunt Hootie. "He usually don't take to strangers."

Suddenly, Buster Junior's much younger alter ego awakened after years of slumber. I didn't even see it coming. He sprang forward and wrapped his crusty front paws around my left leg just above the hem of my plaid Bermuda shorts. As he gained momentum, his humping actually lifted me off the floor. But the harder I tried to pull away, the harder he humped.

"Well, would ya look at that? Buster Junior has a new friend, Mama. That gosh-darn dog must think Jimmy's a girl dog."

"Get that dog off of him, ya hear? I don't want him gettin' no funny ideas."

Is she talking about me or Buster Junior? I wondered. At least I knew which Buster I needed to stay away from.

By day three, Deb and I were starting to get cabin fever, so we talked our father into driving us to the general store down the mountain in Matoaka. He bought all of us Slo Poke suckers, hoping that it would occupy us young'uns for, say, two to three hours. Donny Boy disproved this theory, however, when he fed his to Patsy, the big-uddered family cow. She immediately hacked up her cud, and her large cow eyes rolled back in her head. She was clearly choking to death.

Without hesitation, Aunt Hootie's other grandson, Ronnie

(same mother as Donny Boy, different father), reached into the cow's mouth and pulled the Slo Poke from her throat. She hacked, snorted, belched, and farted, all the time looking a bit embarrassed.

I was awed by my cousin's quick action. Donny Boy was not. "That damn ole cow ate my sucker!" he wailed.

"Now, honey, we'll get you another sucker. I bet Ronnie will give you his," Aunt Hootie said in her comforting voice. Ronnie obliged.

On day four, two days before the big reunion, the smell of chili dogs wafted through the house. I promptly pulled Buster Junior off my leg so I'd be ready when the dinner bell rang.

Clang! Clang! Clang! "Come and get it!"

During the meal, no one said a word. We were too busy eating. Even Donny Boy was relatively quiet, making only the occasional grunting sounds associated with a very large child eating four or five chili dogs at a time with his mouth wide open.

Uncle Homer Joe smiled at his brood and, between bites, said, "Hey, Hootie, tell all these folks how you learned to make such good chili dogs."

"Now, ya ole coot, ya know how I learned to make these here chili dogs," she smiled, waiting for our attention. "Well, ya see, I was workin' at this café down in Matoaka and there was this Russian boy . . . Lord, I think he was Russian . . . maybe he was from Hung'ry or was it Wisconsin? Anyway, his name was Miloslav Krakonavich, and I couldn't understand a word he said. And Lord, oh Lord, did he stink! I don't think that boy *ever* took a bath. Maybe they don't bathe in Russia . . . or Hung'ry . . . or was it Wisconsin?

"Well, anyway, we worked together in this little café down in Matoaka, and one day I said to him, 'Hey, could you teach me how to make them chili dogs?' Now, even though I was married to Homer Joe at the time, I got a bit nervous the way Miloslav turned and looked at me with them ole wonk eyes. They seemed to be lookin' ever'where but *at* me, but, uh-huh I knew what they was tryin' to focus on. He just kept a-smilin' and said, 'I know what you *really* want, Hootie.' I 'bout turned and run out the door, but I needed that job. Plus, I really wanted the recipe for them chili dogs! Well, he was makin' a batch right then, with his pot just a-cookin' away. So you know what he did? He reached his dirty ole hand right down the back of his pants and started diggin' at his butt. Before I knew it, he pulled his hand out and reached right in and grabbed his wienie. . . ."

I almost choked on my chili dog. I quickly looked down the picnic tables to see if others were equally confused. They simply stared at their chili dogs.

"From the pot of boiling water," Hootie chuckled as she continued. "He yanked that ole wienie right out with his bare hand. The *same* hand he used for diggin' at his butt."

"Oh," I said, perhaps a bit disappointed.

"Then he says to me, he says, 'Here Hootie, eat this ole chili dog.' But I says, 'No siree, Miloslav Krakonavich, I ain't eatin' that ole thing . . . uh-uh . . . not after you been a-scratchin' at your butt.'

"Well, ya know, I still took his recipe, and between you, me, and Donny Boy—how ya doin' down there, boy—that's the same recipe I use today."

I was afraid to ask what *her* secret ingredient was.

On day five, my grandmother decided to take Deb and me to visit the abandoned house where my father had been born. It was just on the other side of the mountain, perhaps a half-hour's walk. We were only minutes into our journey when my sister tripped and fell into a small sinkhole. She started screaming hysterically, afraid that Coaldale Mountain was going to swallow her up. Grandma and I pulled as hard as we could, and finally, with a loud *schlurrp*, we were able to extract Deb's bare foot, which had previously sported a brand-new, white canvas PF Flyer. Seeing her shoeless foot only caused her to scream even more.

"Are you hurt?" my grandmother asked, worried.

"No," Deb whined. "But Mom's gonna kill me. She just bought those with her support check."

"Now, hon, your mama ain't gonna kill you over no shoe," Grandma soothed. "Let's just go back to Hootie's. We can go see your Daddy's birthplace some other time."

As we approached the house, someone called my name. I looked over to see several of my cousins gathered around Brownie, the old barnyard mare. With her back bowing sharply downward and her belly almost touching the ground, the poor thing appeared to be in great need of a chiropractor.

"Y'all wanna ride Brownie?" Homer Joe the Second, or Ho Joe as we called him, yelled to me.

When I looked at my grandmother questioningly, she replied, "You ain't never rode no horse, have you?"

"Sure I have. I learned at Scout camp last year."

"Well, alright then. I guess you can ride her. Just don't kill yourself, ya hear?"

It was true that I had gone horseback riding with my Scout troop the previous year, but I'd never ridden bareback before. Even so, with the help of my cousin, I mounted Brownie, which wasn't a difficult task. It was pretty much one leg up and over to settle into Brownie's sagging backbone. I felt oddly secure, I guess because I was pretty much locked in.

Ho Joe handed me the flimsy rope that was masquerading as a rein, then, just as I'd learned at camp, I gently kicked Brownie's sides—or at least where her sides should've been. Improvising, I kicked the dusty ground beneath her ribs and urged her on with a firm, "Giddyup."

That's all it took. Just like that, we were off! Similar to how Buster Junior's alter ego had surfaced a few days earlier, Brownie suddenly came to life. One minute she was simply a tired old horse, the next she had morphed into Triple Crown winner Whirlaway. As we galloped up and over Coaldale Mountain with the whole family yelling, "Stop!" I wondered if Brownie was headed for Kentucky to compete in the Derby. Instead, she decided to show me parts of West Virginia most locals had never seen. We visited neighboring hollows. We climbed mountain trails and visited coal miners in their shafts before wading through rapidly flowing streams and grazing in green pastures. We even raced a '56 Ford Fairlane up a steep, winding road—and won.

Finally, Brownie aka Whirlaway had had enough. She was pooped. Just before reaching the top of the mountain, I saw the remains of an old, abandoned house. *That's where Dad was born,* I thought. I patted the old mare on the head and hugged her

scrawny neck. As we trudged down the other side of the mountain, I saw Ronnie step out from behind the barn. He'd been
waiting for us. He smiled as he took Brownie's rope and led us to
the barn. As we slowed to a stop, he carefully pulled me from the
mass of curved vertebrae that had served as my saddle. He did so
with the same precision and gentleness he'd used when pulling
the Slo Poke from Patsy's throat. Ronnie—always there to lend
a helping hand.

On day six, the family reunion was finally upon us. I took comfort in knowing that in just a couple more days, I'd be home. I
was sure my mother was counting the days too.

That morning, I awoke feeling especially melancholy, wishing my mother were there to visit with and share in the joy of the
family she'd given up. For a while, I sat on the edge of the bed
and looked around the room, not really wanting to face the day.
Everyone else had already gotten up, so it was just me and Buster
Junior. I felt tears welling up in my eyes as I pried the dog off my
leg. I felt so alone.

"Honey, are you okay?"

I jumped and quickly wiped my eyes as Aunt Hootie walked
into the room.

"Jimmy, honey, what's the matter, baby?"

"Uh, nothing."

"Are ya sure, sugar?"

"Uh, yeah, it's just . . . I . . . uh . . . I've got something in
my eye."

"Of course ya do. Can I help ya get it out?"

"Uh, no. . . . I'm okay."

"Okay, precious, just let your ole Aunt Hootie know if ya need some help, ya hear?"

"Yeah, thanks."

When she turned to leave the room, she stopped as if she'd forgotten to tell me something. "Honey, I know you're missin' your mama. And no one knows just how bad you're missin' her 'cept you. And that's okay, baby, that's okay. That shows how much ya love her and worry 'bout her. But, sugar, I've been watchin' for a few days now, and I need to tell ya somethin'. You're carryin' the weight of the world on your shoulders. And you're just too young to be worryin' so much and takin' on ever'one else's problems. Your mama's a big girl, and she's made her decision. It might not be the decision ya want, but it's *her* decision. And y'all have to respect that. It's time to just enjoy bein' a young'un, ya hear?" Aunt Hootie said as she smiled her angelic smile.

I looked out the big window behind her. There, under the shade of an old maple tree, sat my kind, loving, alcoholic grandfather. Covered in the knots and agony of rheumatoid arthritis, he took a quick swig from his bottle of "liquid pain medication." As he placed it back in his pocket, he put his arm around Donny Boy's shoulder and began telling him of his own childhood just over the mountain in a neighboring hollow. Sitting at a nearby picnic table, my angel of a grandmother bathed everyone in her unconditional love as my fun-loving father tickled my bratty sister, who giggled uncontrollably.

I looked up at Aunt Hootie, who was smiling down at me. "Should I try to get that ole thing outta your eye now, so y'all can come out and have some fun with your kinfolk?" She winked at me, then took my hand and led me out of the immaculate room and down the hallway past the living room in all its comic-book glory. As we passed the empty space where the three picnic tables had stood before being moved outside for the reunion, she remarked, "Sure looks bare in here, don't it?"

"Yep. It sure does." When I squeezed her wonderfully soft and loving hand, I felt the warmth of her spirit lift me. Then we went out to greet our family.

Try as
They May

When I was eleven, my dad started dating Earlene, a young widow with three children. The oldest, Becky, had just had her first child at the age of fifteen. J. Lee, the middle child and only son, was thirteen and had a penchant for soaking his already skintight white jeans in hot water to ensure that *nothing* was left to the imagination. The youngest, eleven-year-old Vickie Lynn, wanted desperately to be my best friend—and lover.

Earlene, who originally hailed from Georgia, had married at the tender age of thirteen, had Becky at fourteen, and was a widow with three small children by the time she was eighteen. Her abusive husband had died very tragically—and perhaps, symbolically—after he fell off a church steeple while painting it.

Shortly after his demise, Earlene packed up her three small children and took a Greyhound bus to the land of opportunity and jobs—Elkhart, Indiana—known to many as the RV Capital of the World.

Several years later when Earlene and my dad met, Becky had already gotten married, so it was just Earlene and her two youngest children living in a basement house. What is a basement house, one might ask? Would a person intentionally design and build their dream house in a basement? Probably not, as was the case with this particular house. The answer is quite simple: the builder ran out of funds after the basement floor was poured and the cement block walls were put up, so he added a flat roof with sheets of tar over it and put a For Rent sign out front. It soon became a cozy, underground den for Earlene and her small pack.

When Deb and I were staying with Dad on the weekends, we would often go to the movies or bowling with Earlene and her kids as one big, happy, dysfunctional family. Bowling was always my favorite—not because I liked to bowl or was good at it but because I enjoyed watching J. Lee's backside as he and his tight jeans stealthily made their approach toward the bowling pins. And no one could toss their balls around like J. Lee!

One year, my dad asked my mom if we could spend Thanksgiving with him and Earlene. She begrudgingly gave in. "Hell, yes! Take them! But you'd better not bring them back before Sunday night."

Although I loved to eat, my true excitement stemmed from the fact that I would get to spend the whole day with Tight Pants.

When Deb and I arrived at their underground bunker, I scanned the area, hoping to spot J. Lee, but he wasn't there. *Must be in his room*, I thought—the one he shared with the sump pump. I excused myself and went to the bathroom, praying I would bump into him on the way. I didn't, but I was happy to see some new white jeans soaking in the sink. *The water is still hot, so he must be nearby.*

As I came out of the bathroom and made my way down the pitch-black hallway, I let out a scream when someone grabbed my arm.

"Get your ass in here!" Vickie Lynn ordered as she pulled me into her room and pushed me onto the bed. Although she had scared the bejesus out of me, once I was in her little room, I couldn't help but notice how cheery cement block walls could be when painted hot pink.

"Where's J. Lee?" I casually asked.

"Who gives a shit?" Vickie Lynn shot back. With the mouth of a truck driver, she wasn't one to mince words.

"Well, I thought we could all . . . well, you know . . . maybe play a game of Twister or something," I said hopefully.

"*Twister?* You're fuckin' kiddin' me, right?"

I was mortified not only because she was making fun of me but because she'd used the f-word. It wasn't like I led a sheltered, holier-than-thou life. My parents used their fair share of expletives—usually when yelling at me—but I wasn't even allowed to say the word *fart* until I graduated from college.

Vickie Lynn plopped down next to me on the bed. "Wanna see something?"

"What?" I couldn't help but notice that she'd coyly positioned herself on the bed between me and the door. "Shouldn't we go help with dinner or something?" I asked, stalling for time.

Vickie Lynn laughed as she started gyrating slowly to music only she could hear. "Just keep watchin'." She stood up and made her way around the double bed—not an easy task in a six-by-eight-foot room—then she slithered next to me, slid her hand under her T-shirt, and made circular motions as she neared her chest region. "I'm gettin' titties," she cooed. "Wanna touch 'em?"

God no, I don't want to touch them. I want to play Twister with J. Lee. Where the hell is he?

When Vickie Lynn reached over and touched the thigh of my size 14 husky corduroys, I jerked away.

"Oh, come on," she purred sensually in an eleven-year-old sort of way. "Don't you wanna stick it in?"

"Stick *what* in?" I honestly didn't have a clue what she was talking about. I guess I was a rather naive kid. Even though I'd spent a lot of time at my mom's parents' farm, I honestly thought all the barnyard animals were just playing a weird game of leap-frog as they grunted and carried on. But at this point, I was starting to get *really* nervous.

"Stick your pickle in my cookie," she whispered.

Pickle? Cookie? What is she talking about? I had a pretty good idea, but on the few occasions I'd caught a glimpse of my grand-father's *Playboy* magazines, it looked more like a piece of pie than a cookie.

"Vickie Lynn! Dinner's ready! You and Jimmy come and eat now, ya hear?" Earlene bellowed over the hum of the furnace in the corner of the bedroom. I bolted over Vickie Lynn as she tried to grab me, then I ran down the hallway to the safety of Dad, Earlene, Deb, and J. Lee.

In retrospect, if *J. Lee* had been the one to trap me in his room on that fateful Thanksgiving Day, we might've been really late for dinner.

By the time I hit puberty, I knew I was gay. Although I didn't admit to it for several more years, I had always felt different.

From as far back as I can remember, I had crushes on other boys. But I worked hard at hiding it, fearing that I would be excluded, unfriended, made fun of, or worse yet, disowned.

Looking back, I now realize how obvious it probably was, but those most important to me didn't seem to get it. Unfortunately, a handful of bullies at school did, and they hurled insults and hurtful names my way on a regular basis. Even though I acted like I either didn't hear them or that they didn't bother me, I was dying inside.

During the summer of '69, I became friends with Betty. Although she'd been in my class the previous year, I didn't know her very well. I knew that she'd been held back a year and really struggled with her studies. And because she had a large overbite and had not outgrown the "awkward stage" most kids experience at that age, she was also often the target of bullies.

Like me, Betty found solace at the local roller-skating rink. Neither of us was particularly athletic, but we did get pretty good at skating. After seeing each other frequently at the rink, we developed a friendship of sorts—or so I thought. Betty seemed to want to take it a step further. But the events that unfurled that summer are a prime example of how clueless some people—like Betty, bless her heart—can be. If I had access to her diary, I'm pretty sure it would've read something like this:

From Betty's diary, June 6, 1969:
What a magical day it was yesterday! Love was definitely in the air—along with the scent of pine trees, hot dogs, baked beans, and the nearby swamp—as Jim and I ate our picnic lunches next to a drainage ditch along Oil City Road in Edwardsburg. We had ridden

our bikes there, which was not an easy task. It's not like we don't know how to ride bicycles or anything like that. We just knew that our parents wouldn't let us travel that distance on our Schwinns. Plus, my parents are SOOOO square. I knew they'd freak out if they knew I was meeting my new stud muffin. Jim told his mom that he was working on his Nature merit badge for Boy Scouts, and I told mine that I was going to Laurie's to listen to her new Cowsills' record.

Once we got situated on our sheet, which was much easier to sneak out of the house and carry in my bicycle basket than a blanket, Jim started the campfire. Luckily, we were able to put out the fire quickly before it destroyed all six of those pine trees. It was a good thing the drainage ditch was right there and full of water and that Jim knew how to tie the ankles of his blue jeans into knots and use them like buckets to put out the fire. Of course, he made me cover my eyes when he took off his pants, but I have a confession: I peeked! I've never seen such bright white Fruit of the Looms! Jim is just SO clean!

Anyway, he started the fire again, this time a little closer to the swamp. We roasted our hot dogs using branches from the scorched pine trees because Jim said that's what they do at Boy Scout camp. We also cooked our baked beans right in the can! He is SOOOO smart and manly!!!!

After the hot dogs were done, we started eating. I couldn't help but sense Jim's nervousness as he fidgeted with his wienie. "What's wrong, you groovy dude?" I asked, trying to lighten the mood.

"You really weren't Miss Junior Pear Queen at the Cass County 4-H Fair last year, were you?" he finally asked.

Uh-oh, I thought. Me and my big mouth. Why did I tell him that in the first place? That was last Friday night when we saw each other at our favorite roller-skating and indoor miniature golf hangout, Ho Ching's Rink-N-Sink.

I had just finished eating my fried rice and slice of pizza when Jim glided past me for the first time. From then on, I couldn't keep my eyes off him. I had seen him at school before, but I'd never seen this athletic side of him. After his third or fourth lap without falling, I overheard someone say, "Well, you know, he has his own skates." From that moment on, it was a done deal. I knew I had to have him!

My former best friend had her eye on him too, though. Dumb Dolores, or Dee Dee as I call her, always has been competitive, especially when it comes to something or someone I want. When it was almost time for the ladies' choice skate, I decided to take matters into my own hands. Actually, I took Dee Dee's ponytail into my hand, yanked her into the girls' bathroom, and locked her in a stall. Looking back, that might not have been a nice thing to do, knowing she didn't know how to unlock it from the inside and all, but was it my fault she'd flunked two grades???? Besides, I had only one thing on my mind at that moment: my new dreamboat.

I returned to the rink—thankful that the music was loud enough to drown out Dee Dee's screams—just as

Jim was putting his left foot in, his left foot out, his left foot in, and then shaking it all about. I still can't believe how I went from zero to thirty miles an hour in seconds on skates, screeching to a halt between him and his very favorite thing in the world: the Hokey Pokey. Every eye was on me—except for Dee Dee's, of course. She was still where she deserved to be. I tried to say something to Jim, but the words stuck in my throat. Finally, I was able to mutter the compliment I long to hear someone say to me someday (once my parents get me braces), "You have really nice teeth."

Jim blushed as he kicked his toe stop at the floor. "Awww . . . I bet you say that to all the boys!" Then he sped off and grabbed Bobby Truesdale's hand for the boys-only skate.

But yesterday, sitting there by the drainage ditch amidst the smell of swamp gases and pine needles, I knew I was in big trouble. I had lied. I really wasn't Miss Junior Pear Queen. Mary Jane Hankins was. She had gotten that title fair and square. It was no secret that she'd grown the biggest pear that year.

Desperately seeking to find a way out because I was already head over heels in love with Jim and wanted nothing more than to have him deflower me right there next to the drainage ditch, I nervously quipped, "I'm sorry . . . ha . . . you must've misunderstood. I didn't say I was Miss Junior Pear Queen . . . ha ha. I said I missed Junior Peerkin at the fair. Junior Peerkin is my cousin, and he has the elephant ear and cotton candy stand. He wasn't there this year because his deep fryer and blower thingy are in the shop. Do you know him? . . . You don't? Good . . . uh, I mean, that's too bad. You'd really like Junior and his elephant ears."

    I sure hope Jim bought my story so we can get busy with our wedding plans.

From Jim's journal, June 16, 1969:

What a magical day it was yesterday! I'm in love! I've met the most incredible, wonderful, gorgeous person in the universe. And I still can't believe how much we have in common. We both love skating, going for picnics in the woods, and riding our bikes. But the best part of all is that we're in the same Boy Scout troop! I knew a couple weeks ago when Bobby Truesdale and I skated together for the boys-only skate that we were destined to be together.

    I had seen him at Scouts before, but we're both pretty shy, so we never really talked—until that Friday night when we skated together. And then a few days later, we left for a week at Boy Scout camp. It's funny how fate comes into the picture sometimes. No one else in our troop wanted to share tents with either of us. At least, that's how I interpreted it.

    "I ain't stayin' with that sissy!" yelled Marty Mathison, a pimple-faced know-it-all.

    "He might try to kiss me!" bellowed Tommy Johnson, laughing so hard his huge belly shook.

    "Hey, queer, got a boyfriend yet?" sneered John Epperly, the son of a local minister.

    Finally, Scoutmaster Bates had had it. He put down his fourth s'more, wiped the melted chocolate from his bottom chin, and said, "Now, boys, that's enough. Jim and Bobby, you two can share tent number thirteen down at the far end of the trail."

It was a match made in Boy Scout heaven. We quickly went to work making our tent more homey. Bobby had brought a few accessories and lightweight pictures to soften the rustic feel of the canvas walls. I had brought a whisk broom and dustpan because the one thing I can't stand is a messy tent. Once we were settled into our cozy little nest, we fell into a comfortable routine. We spent hours and hours talking about any- thing and everything—from the color schemes we used when making pot holders with our looms to our favorite outfits for our G.I. Joe and Ken dolls. When the other boys in the troop were out hiking the trails or swimming a mile for their merit badges, Bobby and I would sneak off to the arts and crafts cabin and make wicker baskets and macramé plant holders.

On the third night of our week at Boy Scout camp, with toasted marshmallows on our breath and ghost stories still in our heads, we all headed back to our tents under the light of a full moon. Unlike the previous two nights, this night was muggy and filled with the drone of mosquitoes anxiously awaiting the tasty smorgasbord known as Troop 37.

Once we'd returned to our tent, I didn't want to admit to Bobby that, while packing, I'd stupidly taken my mosquito netting out of my knapsack to make room for the whisk broom, dustpan, and industrial-sized can of Lysol, which had proven to be worth its weight in *gold. After five minutes of me smacking those pesky bug-gers, though, he pulled his own mosquito netting back and said, "Get in here, you!"*

I clumsily crawled out of my sleeping bag and quickly hopped on top of his as he closed the netting. We lay there together, whispering and giggling for hours. At one point, Bobby's hand accidentally slipped down, and he momentarily touched my you-know-what. He seemed a little embarrassed at first—all red-faced and breath-ing hard—but I assured him it was okay. It wasn't his fault anyway. It wasn't like he made my little guy pop out of my pajama bottoms and point in his direction. Accidents like that just happen sometimes.

Just before dawn, I crawled into Bobby's sleeping bag, and, together, we drifted off to sleep.

From Betty's diary, June 21, 1969:
Oh my gosh! Oh my gosh! Oh my GOSH! I got a post-card from my beloved today! I miss him SOOOOOO much! He's been at Boy Scout camp all week, and I feel like I haven't seen him in FOREVER!! He's supposed to come home today, and I just know he can hardly wait to see me! I told my mom and dad I'm going to Laurie's tomorrow, but I'm really going to ride over to Jim's house to surprise him.

From Jim's journal, June 22, 1969:
I got home from camp yesterday, and I miss Bobby SOOOOOO much! I rode my bike to Mrs. McMahon's house today so I could mow her yard, and instead of

coming right home, I snuck over to Bobby's for a while. When I got home, Betty was hiding in the lilac bush behind our house. She scared the crap out of me! I like her, but she won't leave me alone! I know she just wants to be friends, especially since she only has one—or rather, had one. She told me Dolores won't speak to her anymore. She doesn't even know why.

I feel kind of sorry for Betty because the kids are always making fun of her buckteeth. I cringe every time I hear them shout, "Hey, Bucky Betty!" But at least that takes their attention off Pansy Pauley.

And the poor thing is always saying, "When I get my braces . . . ," but her parents sure don't seem to be in any hurry to get her to the orthodontist. Plus, she's always talking about my teeth!

"Oh, Jim, your teeth are so straight!"

"Oh, Jim, you must brush your teeth all the time."

"Oh, Jim, you never get anything stuck in your teeth!"

I appreciate the compliments, but jeez, enough already. Whenever she does it, I try to compliment her back. For instance, today I said, "Periwinkle is a good color on you." She seemed a little embarrassed and turned beet red, so I offered her a Twizzler.

She took it and thanked me. Once she finished chomping, I offered her another, but she declined. At that point, I was just hoping she'd hop on her bike and go home, but instead, she just stood there.

"Wanna play tetherball?" she asked, eyeing my very impressive tetherball court.

I didn't want to play tetherball. I wanted to go back and see Bobby.

As Betty absentmindedly picked at half the Twizzler still lodged in her teeth, she lunged toward me and locked lips with me! I let out a muffled cry and tried to pull away, but her mouth was like a vice grip. Yuck!

From Betty's diary, June 22, 1969:

JIM KISSED ME! Right on the lips! It came out of nowhere. We were just standing there, and before I knew what was happening, our mouths were connected. I have a feeling he's going to be my first!

From Jim's journal, June 23, 1969:

Last night I called Bobby and told him that Betty had kissed me. He's so sweet and understanding and asked if he could come over for a sleepover tonight. When I mentioned it to Mom, she asked, "Who's this Bobby Truesdale?" I had to remind her that he was my best friend. After giving me the third degree about him and his family, she finally agreed. "I just don't want any rowdiness! And make sure his sheets are clean! Do you think he'll want the top or bottom?"

This morning, as I climbed the ladder of my bunk bed to change the sheets, Betty was the furthest thing from my mind—especially since Bobby is coming over tonight! I'm so excited that I feel all jittery and nervous at the same time.

To distract myself and make the time go quicker, I did a deep cleaning of my room and got out my best pajamas.

From Betty's diary, June 23, 1969:

I hope Jim is at the Rink-N-Sink tonight! Mom said I could wear some eyeliner and lipstick! Well, she didn't actually say that, but I don't think she'll mind after she finds out Jim and I are going steady.

From Jim's journal, June 24, 1969:

I can't EVEN believe how lucky I am! When Bobby got here yesterday, Mom made us some popcorn, and we watched That Girl *and* Bewitched. *It's so weird how we like the same stuff! Later, we watched* Night Gallery, *but Mom said we had to go to bed if we didn't stop screaming. When we finally went to my room, I told Bobby the sheets were clean on the top bunk. He was kind of quiet for a few seconds, then he said, "Can I tell you a secret and you'll promise not to laugh?" I just wanted to give him a great big hug right then and there, so I did. He looked at me with his beautiful blue eyes and whispered, "I'm afraid of heights." I couldn't help myself and hugged him again. He clung to me for what seemed like an eternity. When we slowly pulled away from each other, I did what any good host would do: I took his hand and led him to the bottom bunk.*

From Betty's diary, June 24, 1969:

Last night was the worst! Not only was my dreamboat not at the Rink-N-Sink, but I also got grounded for wearing eyeliner and lipstick. My parents are SO square! Don't they realize that Jim and I are in love?

I need to go make sure he's okay! What if something horrible has happened to him???

From Jim's journal, June 25, 1969:

Something wonderful has happened to me! Bobby! He's just so cute! And SO sweet! We were awake most of the night talking. Then, when we finally tried to go to sleep, we were both so hot, being together in that little bed and all. We took off all the blankets, but even that didn't work. So we ended up taking off our pajama bottoms, and before we knew it, we were sleeping like babies. But when we woke up, I was really embarrassed because I had a boner. It was almost like Bobby could read my mind, though, because he reassured me that it was okay. To make me feel better, he told me he had one too. Isn't that weird how we both had boners at the same time?

From Betty's diary, June 26, 1969:

I want so much for my first time with Jim to be majorly special. I almost wish I'd let Dennis Walton go all the way with me last year when we snuck into the boiler room during fifth hour. At least I'd know what I was supposed to do. But that stupid Mr. Robbins just had to walk in and find us. And he didn't even buy Dennis's story that he was doing a special credit project for Building Trades. How were we supposed to know there's no filter to change on a boiler? But, then again, Dennis is pretty dumb. He's flunked even more times than Dee Dee has!

From Jim's journal, June 26, 1969:

Uh-oh. Betty is getting really weird. Now she's started calling me! Yesterday, she called like five times! I'm afraid to even answer the phone anymore. Last night, Mom said, "Who the hell keeps calling?" I told her it was someone from school. Then she asked if it was that girl who could eat corn through a picket fence, whatever that means. I only answer the phone now because it could be Bobby.

From Betty's diary, June 27, 1969:

Jim and I talk on the phone ALL the time! It's like we can't get enough of each other! I know my honey feels the same way about me that I feel about him, but I'm getting really tired of him and that prissy Bobby Truesdale always doing things together. I know Jim is only spending time with him because he feels sorry for that weirdo. I love that part about my sweetie, but enough already. We only have a few more weeks before we go back to school, and even though I'm going to sign up for all the same classes as Jim, we need to spend every moment we can together.

From Jim's journal, June 28, 1969:

Bobby's parents are going out of town for three days, and they asked my mom if he could stay with us! Mom said YES! I am SOOOOOO excited!!! I'm going to clean my room really well today and change the sheets on the bottom bunk, since we won't need the top one. I thought about getting some new pajamas, but that would be dumb because we'd just end up taking them off anyway.

YAY! My Bobby is coming tomorrow and staying three whole days!!!

From Betty's diary, June 28, 1969:

Dee Dee called and asked if we were still friends. I told her I wasn't sure after what she did to me. She said, "I didn't do anything to you!" So I reminded her of why I was forced to lock her in the stall. After she remembered, I said we were friends again. Kinda sorta. She's really dumb, so I explained very slowly that Jim and I are going steady and plan to get married. Then she said, "Well, aren't Jim and Bobby Truesdale really, really, really good friends?" Boy, is she lucky we were on the phone and not together, or I would've locked her in the bathroom stall again!

From Jim's journal, July 2, 1969:

I know now what true love feels like! Actually, I know what a lot of things feel like now. The last few days have been the best! Bobby and I just can't seem to get enough of each other. Mom asked if we were feeling okay because we kept taking naps. At least that's what she thought we were doing. She also said, "Why don't you boys go outside for a while? What in the world can you do in that bedroom for so long?"

On the first night, after we took off our pajama bottoms, it happened again. Boner City! We knew then and there we had to take matters into our own hands. So we did. We took matters into our own hands—and then each other's hands. Afterward, we both felt much better.

But then the next night the same thing happened.
And again last night.

From Betty's diary, July 2, 1969:

I HATE Bobby Truesdale! I hope he falls backward on
his skates and hits his head and goes into a coma. That
would serve him right!

Jim wants to spend all his time with that uggo!
What's he got that I don't have, for crying out loud! It's
not like I'm getting any younger! I guess I'll just have
to be patient. Dad and Mom told me I have to at least
try to finish high school before Jim and I get married.
I know that deep down Jim feels the same way as me,
but he's too shy to say anything. I wonder what he and
Stupid Bobby talk about, if they even talk.

From Jim's journal, June 7, 1974:

I wish I was more excited about graduating tomorrow. I
mean, I'm looking forward to college and all, but I wish
Bob and I were going to the same school. At least we can
write to each other, and Christmas break will be here
before we know it. This will be the longest we've ever
gone without seeing each other. I don't know how I'm
going to do it. I'm going to miss him so much!

From Betty's diary, June 7, 1974:

I can't believe I'm actually graduating tomorrow,
despite what Mom, Dad, and all my teachers said.
Well, at least I will be graduating once I go to summer
school for the three classes I flunked this semester. Dee

Dee dropped out last year and got a job at the Whip-N-Dip, and she said she was sure she could get me a job there too. She said the job is pretty easy. You just need to know the difference between chocolate and vanilla ice cream. Duh! Once I start working, I can save money for when my Jim comes to his senses and asks me to visit him at college. At least he won't be anywhere near that stupid Bob, who I hope falls down two flights of stairs and breaks every bone in his body and never walks again.

And if Jim doesn't come to his senses before then, I'll get to see him over Christmas. I'll sneak over and surprise him as much as I can.

I'm going to miss him so much!

From Jim's journal, July 14, 1979:

I had a great time at our five-year class reunion! It seemed almost surreal being back there after so many years. I still recognized almost everyone. Well, except for Betty. When she tapped me on the shoulder, I had no idea who she was. Until she smiled, that is. She was already a little tipsy, but she got even tipsier throughout the evening. And every time I turned around, there she was, handing me her phone number.

The best part of the evening, though, was seeing Bob again. I couldn't take my eyes off him, and a couple of times, I caught him staring at me. We haven't seen each other for a few years, and we've kind of lost touch. I'm so glad I came out to my parents last year. I don't have to hide anything anymore. And even though Bob and

*I are both with someone now, we've decided to stay in
touch. He really was one of the best friends I've ever had.
I'm feeling so good right now!*

From Betty's diary, July 14, 1979:

*My dream is finally coming true! My beloved Jim was at
the reunion, and HE IS SOOOOOOO HOT! He played
this little game with me when he first saw me, pretend-
ing like he didn't know who I was. When I reminded
him of our plans to marry, it was almost like he didn't
even hear me. I wonder if he's going deaf. And he kept
looking across the room and smiling at that idiot Bob
Truesdale. He thinks he's really something, that guy! I
asked Jim if we could at least set a date, since I want
to get my braces and lose some weight and stuff before
the wedding. Again, he didn't even respond. He just
kept staring over my shoulder. I gave him my number a
couple of times, just in case he might've lost it.*

*I hated having to leave at ten o'clock, but that's
when my lame parents insisted on picking me up. And
they threatened to ground me for drinking! I'm SO tired
of hearing, "While you're living under our roof, you
will follow our rules!" Oh brother. It's not like I'm not
supporting myself.*

*Oh! I told Jim I can come visit for the whole winter
if he'd like since Whip-N-Dip is closed then. He didn't
say anything, so I'm pretty sure he's trying to figure it
all out.*

*Last week, Dee Dee told me she thought Jim and
Bob might be queers. She's lucky she didn't have a*

ponytail when she told me that or I would've yanked her right back into another bathroom stall and locked the door. Besides, even if Jim thinks he might be gay, I know I can change him.

I'm feeling so good right now!

Fast forward to September of 1984. It was my twenty-eighth birthday, and I had a lot to celebrate, especially this particular year with so many good things happening. My partner, Rich, and I had just bought our first house, which was another coming out of sorts. For the few people who might not have known or accepted that we were gay, buying a house together should've left no room for doubt . . . or so one would think.

On the morning of my birthday, having been forced to celebrate a little bit too much the night before, I was really hoping just to stay snuggled up in bed next to my love. The telephone ringing loudly on my bedside table changed all that, though. I ignored it the first two times, but when it started ringing again, I grabbed it.

"HELLO!" I yelled into the phone.

"A happy birthday to you,
A happy birthday to you,
May each da-ay of the year,
May you fa-hind Jesus here.
A happy birthday to you,
A happy birthday to you,
The-uh best year you've everrrr had!"

"Hi, Sister Dawson."

"Well, praise Jesus, how in the good Lord's name did ya know it was me?"

"A wild guess?"

"Well, I just wanted to call and wish a happy birthday to my very favorite nephew-in-law-to-be—once he marries my niece Dorothy, that is! Hallelujah!"

"Thanks."

"How you doin', sweetheart? Are you takin' good care of yourself and your temple?"

"My what?"

"You know, your temple . . . your *body*! It's written right there in the holiest of books, 'Know ye not that your body is the temple of the Holy Ghost which is in you, which ye have of God, and ye are not your own.' *Praise the Lord! Sweet Jesus!* First Corinthians, chapter six, verse nineteen. *AMEN!*"

I wasn't sure how to respond to this. My "temple" was rebelling big-time that morning, primarily from the alcohol I'd consumed just a few hours earlier. As a matter of fact, if I recall correctly, my temple was majorly pissed off at me right then.

Had I known my Bible verses better, I would've responded, "'Drink no longer water, but use a little wine for thy stomach's sake and thine often infirmities.' First Timothy, chapter five, verse twenty-three. *Praise Jesus!*"

"Now, honey," Sister Dawson continued, "have you been readin' that ole Bible I gave you a few years ago?"

"I, uh—"

"You know, the one that I took the liberty of writin' all my own thoughts in, so you wouldn't find it too confusin' or have to ever try to figure out anythin' for yourself. It's all right there

for you: the truth, accordin' to our precious heavenly father—
and me. Amen!"

"How's Dorothy?" I felt I should ask.

"Dorothy Sue is fine. She said she feels like an old maid.
She just turned thirty, poor baby. She's not gettin' any younger,
Mr. Jim. No sirree, someone best be gettin' a move on it! Now,
mind you, I'm not tryin' to get pushy, it's just that ever since
the revival when Dottie Sue—I'm the only one she lets call
her Dottie Sue, but I sure bet she'd let you call her that, too, if
you ever took a hankerin'. Anyway, after that old revival when
she had her rebirth as I like to call it, she's been havin' visions
of her weddin'. Oh, and what a beautiful bride she says she'll
be. Since she quit cuttin' her hair after the revival, she won't
even need a train for her bridal gown. Nope, uh-uh, she'll just
have those glorious locks flowin' right down the aisle behind
her. Only thing is, you—I mean, the man *lucky* enough to be
marryin' that little dumplin'—would have to be *very* careful
not to step on them. Wouldn't that be an awful mess? My beautiful niece trippin' at her own weddin'. But you—I mean, the
man *lucky* enough to be marryin' her—would catch her just
before she hit the biggest weddin' cake you ever did see! And
do you know how I know that? Because I have my own visions.
That's my gift.

"Are you surprised that your former Sunday school teacher
remembers your birthday? Lord, I can't even recollect where I
put my Phillips' Milk of Magnesia half the time, let alone remem-
berin' birthdays. How old were you when you started comin' to
my class? Do you remember how we used to play Bible bingo?"

I did remember. Actually, that's why I went to her class. I
usually walked out with a shitload of 3 Musketeers bars.

"Genesis four! Deuteronomy twenty-three! Revelations thirty-seven! Obadiah fifty-six! Lamentations sixty-five! '*Bible bingo!* Sister Dawson, I got me a Bible bingo!' Oh, praise the Lord, Jimmy, that was music to my ears. I sure do miss those days, don't you, honey?"

I missed the 3 Musketeers bars.

"Do you remember that little twinkie boy that always came with you? What was his name? Barry, Larry, Harry, or somethin' like that?"

"It was Gary."

"That's it! Sweet Jesus, I've always prayed for that little fruit-cake. What his parents must've gone through, knowin' they'd brought somethin' like that into the world. An abomination. Oh Lord, have mercy on his wicked little soul."

The conversation, or should I say Sister Dawson's monologue, suddenly came to an end—*praise the Lord!*

"Well, sweetheart, it sure has been fun catchin' up with you. I always tell Dottie Sue, 'That Jim, whoo-ee, what a talker!' And the way you used to recite the books of the Bible. Just shows you what a little love can do to teach a child—and 3 Musketeers bars. Ha ha!"

Her voice took on a serious tone as she said, almost scold-ingly, "Darlin', you need to give Dottie Sue a call soon. Oh Lord, I see it all as clear as I see this old wart on my chin ever' mornin'. You two are meant for each other. You take care now. I love you, sugar."

Oh Lord was right. I dragged myself out of bed, knowing damn well my temple was wide awake at that point. I tried to be quiet so I wouldn't disturb my homosexual abomination of a partner. *Praise Jesus!*

Too late. "Who's Sister Dawson?" he asked groggily.

"My old Sunday school teacher."

"Oh brother," he said, his eyes probably rolling under his closed lids.

"No, it's Sister . . . *Sister* Dawson," I corrected as he reached out and pulled me back under the covers to commit some act that would no doubt pave my path straight to eternal damnation.

Bitten by
the Bug

From the moment I popped into the world, I was a consummate dreamer. And being somewhat of a loner growing up, I had plenty of time to do just that. As far back as I can remember, one of my biggest dreams was to travel all over the world.

I spent countless hours poring over the world atlas that came with our Encyclopedia Britannica. Whenever I'd find an exceptionally interesting or exotic place, I'd dig into the encyclopedia and read anything and everything I could about it. Then I'd escape into my own little dream world.

One moment I might find myself lounging on a remote island in Fiji, the next playing with kangaroos in the Australian outback. From there, I'd suddenly be teleported to Kenya, looking all dapper in my safari attire. And sometimes, while completely lost in my own imagination, I could almost *hear* the crackling of a roaring fire in an Alpine lodge after a strenuous, yet pleasurable, day skiing the Matterhorn. In my make-believe world, I've gambled at casinos in Monaco, gone on archaeological digs in Egypt, walked the ancient streets of Jerusalem, trekked to Machu Picchu, and sipped champagne with the Eiffel Tower as my backdrop.

I'm very grateful to have had parents who never squelched my often far-fetched dreams. I'm sure at times they wanted to laugh out loud when I voiced some of my most outlandish aspirations, but, instead, they supported and encouraged me to make my dreams a reality.

At the start of my freshman year of high school, I was beyond excited to hear that the German teacher, Fräulein Schneider, was taking a small group of students to Germany and Austria during spring break. Although I had never studied German, I knew it would be the opportunity of a lifetime. And because my best friend, Bobby, had already signed up for the trip, I *had* to go! Unfortunately, this was one of the times my mother did not support and encourage me.

"I don't have seven hundred dollars for that!" she exclaimed.

I was crushed.

"If you save the money, you can go in two years," Mom said because I had stupidly told her they made the trip every other year.

"In *two* years? But I wanna go now! With Bobby! *His* parents are paying for it!" I screamed, perhaps a bit too loudly.

"Don't yell at me, young man! And good for him, but you're not Bobby, and I'm not paying for it. It sounds like a wonderful trip, so if it's really that important to you, start saving your money now."

I knew there was no swaying her, so I quieted down and decided to move on to Plan B: I'd ask my dad to pay for the trip. Or, more specifically, I would *guilt* my dad into paying for it. When I wanted something badly enough, I knew just how to work him. I would bring up the divorce and allow my voice to crack and tremble at exactly the right moment. It rarely failed.

Unfortunately, this time it *did* fail because Mom was well aware of how I operated, and she got to Dad first.

"Your mom and I think it would be best if you save the money and pay for it yourself. It will help you learn about responsibility."

I didn't want to learn about responsibility. I *wanted* to go to Germany!

But I had no choice. When I turned fourteen at the end of September, I was able to get a work permit, so I took a weekend job as a dishwasher at a local restaurant. And for the next two years, I did every odd job I could find. I cleaned garages, mowed and weeded lawns, washed cars, and babysat. I even painted my grandparents' living room.

The summer before my sixteenth birthday, Dad bought a new car, so I asked what he was going to do with his like-new '67 Olds Cutlass. He said he planned on selling it, so I hinted very strongly that I would love to have it. He agreed and said he would only charge me four hundred dollars for it rather than the eight hundred he hoped to get. He obviously didn't understand when I said I would love to *have* it, so I tried to explain. But he sat me down and did his own explaining. He reasoned that me paying for it would be yet another lesson in learning responsibility. I was already getting really sick of responsibility.

I reluctantly paid for the car out of my Germany fund and moved it into my mom's garage. I was still a couple months shy of my sixteenth birthday, so I spit shined and detailed it frequently and backed it in and out of the garage a few dozen times a day for practice.

On my birthday, Dad arrived at our house shortly after I got home from school. Then he drove me in the Cutlass to the license bureau where I was scheduled to take my driving test. I passed with flying colors, so once I took Dad back to Mom's house, I headed to a local grocery store and applied for a job. I'd heard it paid better than my dishwashing job, and I finally had the wheels to get to and from there.

For the next several months, I bagged groceries and stocked shelves every evening after school and on the weekends. Between that and studying, I didn't have much of a life, but I was determined to go to Germany! That was my goal.

The following March, my dream came to fruition. Along with Fräulein Schneider and several other students—whose *parents* had paid for them to go—I flew to Munich and spent the next eight days exploring Germany and Austria.

On the first night, Fräulein Schneider took us to an authentic German restaurant. She wanted us to sample all the local dishes. She even said we could each have a small beer. But before eating or drinking anything, we were given a quick language lesson on proper pronunciation. Once we said each item correctly, we were allowed to partake. The word for beer (*Bier*) was a piece of cake, but the word for piece of cake was a totally different story.

"*Shhvarts-vail-dare-keersh-tort-eh!*" she repeated over and over and over, enunciating each and every syllable with great precision, which, in German, equates to a *lot* of syllables.

After dinner, we visited another of Munich's trademarks: Hofbräuhaus, one of the oldest breweries in Germany and a major tourist attraction. It's been around since the 1500s. We were wide-eyed as we entered. Long tables were filled with people in the huge, noisy hall. Some patrons were actually dancing on the tables while waitresses in traditional Bavarian outfits juggled up to ten huge steins of beer at a time.

Fräulein found us a spot at a table and said, "You can each have one if you remember how to pronounce it."

"*BIER!*" we screamed in unison.

Even though I was only sixteen, I wasn't a total stranger to beer. My mother's father had often given me a small glass while he was enjoying his nightly two bottles. But I had never had a full liter of any beer, let alone German beer. None of us had. A few couldn't take more than a sip or two. Others gulped it down. I was kind of in the middle, between the sippers and the gulpers.

After Fräulein finished hers, she looked around the table then leaned over and whispered in my ear. "If I go back to the hotel, would you keep an eye on everyone and don't stay out too late? I'm trusting you because you seem very responsible."

This responsibility gig was getting to be a lot of work.

After she left, I bought another round for the gulpers. We emptied those then decided it would be a good idea to dance on the tables like so many others were doing. We moved and stomped to the *oompah-pah* of the polka band until we couldn't move or stomp anymore. The gulpers finished the sippers' beers before we staggered back to our hotel.

When Fräulein woke us early the next morning, many of us were suffering from our first hangovers. But we were scheduled for another day of touring, specifically Neuschwanstein Castle, located deep in the heart of Bavaria. On the two-hour bus ride there, we had more language lessons.

"*Noy-shhvon-shhtine! Noy-shhvon-shhtine!*"

After repeating it several times, some of us started nodding off, but Fräulein Schneider wouldn't allow it. "*Nein! Nein!*" she yelled, her own accent peeking through. "No shhleeping today!"

She then walked up and down the aisle, tapping our heads to ensure that none of us missed any of the incredible scenery.

Thankfully, I was wide awake when we neared our destination because my first glimpse of that beautiful castle situated in the majestic mountains truly was breathtaking. It was something I'll always remember. I immediately understood Fräulein's passion and love for languages and all things foreign.

In the fall of 1973, during my senior year of high school, I was balancing school and work at the grocery store and still tooling around in my '67 Olds Cutlass. In December, my mother's parents, who wintered in southern Texas, came back for Christmas. One day, I overheard my grandmother tell my mother that although she loved the climate of southern Texas, she was extremely lonely and homesick while they were there.

Later when I was alone with her, I said, "Grammy, maybe I can come down for a visit over my spring break." I knew my grandma would love that, but I also knew my mother wouldn't allow me—at seventeen years old—to drive that distance alone. But given my newfound knowledge of responsibility, I continued with what I was pretty certain would get the perfect reaction. "But I don't think Mom will let me drive that far." For effect, I looked down at my feet, trying to appear as sad as I possibly could.

"Let me talk to her!" Grammy said, suddenly brightening up.

I truly was a responsible teenager. I was a good student, never broke curfew, helped around the house, and because I was so busy with work and school, I hardly had time to pick on my little brother.

My plan worked like a charm, and Mom reluctantly agreed to let me do it. I'm sure she would've said no if she hadn't seen how excited her mother was about the prospect of a visitor. Mom had one stipulation, though. I had to find another very responsible person to accompany me. I thought about it for several weeks, knowing I had to make the right choice for it to work. Or, more specifically, for Mom to allow it. My first pick was Bobby, of course, but I already knew he was going to Florida with his parents. So I ended up asking a classmate named Dave—a quiet, bookish sort of guy. He seemed a bit surprised when I presented him with my offer. Truth be told, we weren't exactly friends—heck, we barely even knew each other aside from having two classes together. But I was pretty sure my mom would approve of him.

Our parents didn't really know each other either, but they met and discussed our trip. It was a rather big deal for two seventeen-year-olds to embark on an adventure like that, but they finally agreed.

My next step was to ask my boss for time off over spring break. I'd recently been promoted to sausage maker, a skill few had at that particular store. I hoped the sausage lovers of Edwardsburg could survive with me gone for nine days. But when I told my boss where I was going, he was thrilled.

"You'll love Texas! And that'll be during Mardi Gras! You'll be so close—you've *gotta* go to New Orleans! We went last year and loved it. If you do go—since it's right across the border from Texas—you should stay at the Marriott on Canal Street. Oh, and have breakfast at Brennan's and dinner at the Court of Two Sisters." He snapped his fingers and said, "I'll tell you what! If you promise to stay at the Marriott and go to Brennan's and the Court of Two Sisters, I'll pay for it!"

That was a much better stipulation than my mom's earlier one.

As spring break neared, I decided I'd better get to know Dave better. At this point, all I really knew for sure was that he was a good student, he was very clean-cut, and he had his driver's license. Those seemed like important criteria for such a long road trip, but aside from that, I knew very little. *What snacks does he like? What's his favorite drink? Does he prefer to do most of the driving? Is he even a good driver? Does he like Neil Diamond, Sonny and Cher, Cat Stevens, Uriah Heep, Patsy Cline, Mac Davis, Aerosmith, Rod Stewart, Tony Orlando and Dawn, Deep Purple, Loretta Lynn, Simon & Garfunkel, and the Polka Family Band as much as I do?* The latter question was especially important since I'd just had a new Sony cassette player and speakers installed.

And after we arrive in Texas, will we share a bed? I wondered. My grandma had told me Dave and I would be staying in a small efficiency apartment on the property where their trailer was parked. *If we do share a bed, does Dave wear pajamas? Does he like to sleep in? Does he shower in the morning or evening? Does he like to watch TV?* I had so many unanswered questions.

Even if Dave and I had very little in common, he was Mom-approved and the trip was quickly approaching. In retrospect, the one thing I should've done beforehand was go on a test-drive with him.

We left early on a Friday morning in March, with me at the wheel. It was still dark outside, and the snow that was falling when we left soon became a blizzard—a total whiteout. With only one lane usable on the highway, I followed an 18-wheeler, white-knuckled, for the next four hours. When I was finally able to pull into a truck stop, the snow had slowed considerably, but I needed a break. Dave and I went inside and used the facilities, and on the walk back to the car, I asked if he minded driving for a while. He turned to me, somewhat surprised, and said matter-of-factly, "I don't know how to drive a stick." Had the weather not been so bad between us and home, I might've turned around right then and there. But I didn't want to admit that I'd screwed up, so I got behind the wheel and continued driving while Dave got in the back seat and stretched out with the pillow and blanket he'd brought. I popped a Cat Stevens tape in my new cassette player and hit PLAY, in hopes that it would calm my frazzled seventeen-year-old nerves.

"Turn that damn thing down!" Dave screamed from the back seat like a curmudgeonly old man.

It's going to be a long trip, I silently groaned to myself.

Twenty-eight hours to be exact. That's how long it took me to drive straight through. Occasionally, Dave would say something from the back seat, but aside from that and a barely audible Mac Davis, Patsy Cline, or Rod Stewart, it was a quiet trip. We arrived around ten on Saturday morning, and although I wanted nothing more than to sleep for two days, my grandparents had other plans. They had a lot to show us. And they did. Besides all the local sights, we spent a day in Matamoros, Mexico, before taking a two-day trip to San Antonio. There, we went to the rodeo, River Walk, and visited the Lone Star Brewery. Our five days in Texas flew by, and before we knew it, we were once again in the Cutlass, en route to New Orleans and Mardi Gras.

As I studied my atlas while Dave made his nest in the back seat, I suddenly realized that geography wasn't my boss's best subject because 683 miles isn't exactly what I would call "so close" or "right across the border." But since I'd already promised my boss to go there and he'd already given me the money, off we went.

Dave and I started out early and arrived in New Orleans around four that afternoon. Although our hotel was close to downtown, it took us another hour to get there. Despite the fact that I was quickly becoming an experienced driver, I was still a bit green when it came to city driving. Plus, several streets had been closed for the festivities, and there were people everywhere! I was still a bit naive, so I assumed that Mardi Gras was just one big parade that started at a certain time and ended a couple of hours later.

Boy, was I wrong!

When we finally reached the hotel's parking garage, I was exhausted yet excited to be in New Orleans. Dave, who didn't seem as excited, informed me that he was glad we were there because, "The back seat is really uncomfortable!"

Like the streets, the hotel lobby was filled with costumed revelers. Dave and I checked in and took the elevator to our room. It was the nicest hotel I had ever seen, and the room was beautiful. But I couldn't wait to get out to the crowded streets and experience something new. Dave, on the other hand, couldn't wait to turn on the TV.

"Are you coming to the French Quarter with me?" I asked, stunned by his lack of interest.

"What? With all those *people*? Are you crazy? I'm not goin' out there!"

Maybe I *was* crazy, but I had a lot of new things to experience! And this seventeen-year-old country boy was about to experience things he'd never even imagined. By the time I got downstairs, people were lining the streets, waiting anxiously for the floats to start passing by. As the first one came into view, those in the crowd went wild, screaming and waving their arms in the air. The costumes, worn by both onlookers and those on the floats, were incredible. As the frenzied crowd got drunker and louder, inhibitions were thrown aside. Thousands of strands of beads were tossed from the floats, and everyone tried to catch them. Some of the women raised their tops, while others—both men and women—removed their clothes completely. My eyes were darting everywhere—I couldn't take it all in fast enough.

After the parade ended, I tried to make my way down Bourbon Street. Laden with my newly acquired beads, I quickly learned to simply go with the flow of the crowd of drunk people. And as I moved upstream, I suddenly got pushed into a packed bar. I looked around, wondering if I'd get carded if I ordered a hurricane, but before I could even get to the bar, someone handed me one. Inebriated people can be so generous.

I took a sip of my hurricane and tried not to make a face. After I took a couple more sips, then a couple more, it started tasting better, and I was starting to feel really, really good. I finished the drink and made my way through the throng to the bar. Still not sure if I'd get carded, I ordered another hurricane. A few minutes later, as I groped my way to the exit with my second hurricane in hand, I couldn't help but think just how responsible I'd become.

I knew the sensible thing would be to head back to the hotel, but the flow of people moving in the opposite direction thought differently, so I continued my journey down Bourbon Street. That night, I witnessed everything imaginable—and some things quite unimaginable. People stood on the small wrought iron balconies of the buildings lining the street, mooning and flashing the crowd below. Then, as I passed a gaggle of drag queens, outrageously dressed with their hair three feet high, one grabbed my arm and said, "Honey, wouldn't you like a piece of this?" I was shocked and mesmerized at the same time.

Suddenly, without warning, I was sucked into another club. I needed a third drink, so I searched the crowded, smoky room for the bar. That's when I spotted the small, brightly lit stage at the back of the room. Gazing through the haze of smoke, I wondered if my eyes were playing tricks on me. I saw two people—a man and a woman—onstage, and both were naked. It took a moment for me to register that they were engaged in something I'd previously only witnessed the barnyard animals doing on my grandparents' farm. I watched for several minutes, just to make sure they were doing what I thought they were doing. Certain that they were, I made my way to the exit. By this time, the streets were less crowded, so I headed back to the hotel, where I found Dave fast asleep.

A few hours later, we were both up. We were also hungry, even though I wasn't feeling the greatest from what was then my second hangover. But I had promised my boss that we'd have breakfast at Brennan's.

Later that evening, we had an early dinner at the Court of Two Sisters, partly because Dave wanted to get back to the hotel in time to watch *The Waltons*, partly because I couldn't wait to have another hurricane and watch naked people doing it onstage, and partly because I had a long drive home the next day.

We left early the next morning, just hours after I'd returned to the hotel. As we drove down the littered streets, where cleaning crews picked up debris, I felt both happy and sad—sad that I was leaving but happy for experiencing the magic of Mardi Gras. Right then, I made a vow to myself that I'd someday return.

I wondered what Dave was feeling in the back seat, but before I could wonder too long, he grumbled like a grandpa, "Turn that damn music down!"

I took Simon & Garfunkel down a notch and bade farewell to the Big Easy.

In my freshman year of college, studying a foreign language was a requirement for all students. Only those who had several years of another language in high school and had passed a proficiency exam were exempt. Even though I had gone to Germany and felt like I was an expert in all things German, my vocabulary was rather limited. True, the words *Bier, Hofbräuhaus, Neuschwanstein,* and *Schwarzwälder Kirschtorte* now rolled off my tongue, but I had a feeling my professors probably wouldn't consider me fluent. We had the choice of French, Spanish, Russian, German, or Latin. I, of course, chose German, what with my connection and all. But for reasons that elude me to this day, I also decided to take Spanish at the same time.

I loved them both from the very start. So much, in fact, that I joined the German and Spanish clubs. Both groups met once a week, usually for dinner. Several club members were already in their second, third, or fourth year of the language, and the goal was to speak only that language during the meetings. It was a great learning experience for those of us who were just beginning. At first, us neophytes were rather quiet, but over time, we started feeling more comfortable conversing in that specific language—or at least attempting to do so.

Toward the end of my first semester, Herr Rottenbiller,

the head of the German department, approached me with an offer. Knowing that I was excelling in German and already had the desire to make it my major, he said there was going to be a vacancy in the German section of the International House, a new, modern structure that housed language majors and foreign exchange students. There were three different sections—German, Spanish, and French—and the concept was that those living there immerse themselves in the particular language or languages they were studying. I felt like I'd hit the jackpot! I quickly accepted and was even happier to find out that I'd be rooming with a German exchange student. I figured that if he was any fun at all, he could teach me all kinds of dirty expressions.

The college also offered several excellent off-campus programs. From the moment I first heard about these, I was hell-bent on spending a semester each in Guadalajara, Mexico, and Heidelberg, Germany, during my junior year.

For the next year and a half, I worked my *Arsch* off. I took a job with the food service department at the college, working every meal of the day and going to classes in between. While at home over the next two summers, I worked in factories and tried to save money for my junior year abroad. I had been accepted to both programs and would be spending the first semester in Guadalajara and the second semester in Heidelberg.

When I arrived in Guadalajara at the end of August 1976, I lived with an older woman in a quiet neighborhood. Although Mamáne lived alone, she had several children and grandchildren nearby. On my first day there, Mamáne made a nice dinner for me, so in my best Spanish, I attempted to tell her she was a good cook.

"*Que buena cochina!*" I said, proud of myself for saying something without having to reference my pocket *diccionario*.

She promptly spit out her food and started choking as she pounded the table. I jumped up, thinking she was dying, but she waved me away. She finally calmed down and through her laughter, she said in broken English, "I theenk jew trrry to tell me I am good cook?"

"*Sí,*" I said, nodding my head.

Mamáne started laughing all over again before continuing, "You tell me I'm a peeg! . . . But a good peeg!"

I almost died right there on the spot. I had never been so embarrassed in my *vida*. Well, at least not until later when her grandson, who was my age, told me that in slang what I'd said meant, "You are a good fuck!" That surpassed my earlier embarrassment by leaps and bounds.

Over the next few months, Mamáne told the story many more times. And each time, as she wiped the tears from her face, she said, "But at least he said I was a good one!" I still hope she meant pig.

While in Mexico, Señor Ortiz, the director of our study abroad program there, felt that although classes were important, traveling throughout different parts of Mexico would also be a valuable learning experience. Shortly after we'd arrived, Mexico had a sudden devaluation of the peso against the US dollar. As sad as it was for the citizens, it was extremely beneficial for those of us studying there because what we'd expected to pay for tuition and housing was cut in half, which allowed Señor Ortiz to take us on several road trips. We saw mummies in Guanajuato, had beach time in Puerto Vallarta, rode on a *trajinera* boat through the floating gardens of Xochimilco, went horseback riding in Michoacán, and climbed the pyramids of Teotihuacán.

The semester ended much too quickly, and I returned to Michigan for Christmas. I was only home for two weeks before leaving on yet another adventure, this time in Germany.

Just like there had been in Mexico, eight students from my college were studying abroad in Heidelberg. We all arrived on various flights at different times. Herr Köhler (or Hair Curler, as we called him), the study abroad director in Germany, met my flight in Frankfurt. I quickly understood the meaning of culture shock when he spoke only German to me. Although I had studied it for two years in college at that point, I had just spent the last four months immersed in the Spanish language.

Maybe it was because I was young and so excited to learn, or maybe it was because my German host family didn't speak a word of English, but what was stored in my memory bank rapidly resurfaced. And then I promptly started learning more. It's not that I am or ever was a quick study, it was more of a sink or swim situation: learn or never understand a word anyone was saying.

Being pale-skinned with blue eyes, I was often mistaken for a native, so the locals always spoke German to me. Within a week, I was trying to only converse *auf Deutsch*, other than occasionally breaking into my mother tongue with my fellow American students.

My classes were very intense that semester, and even after I finished them, I still had a few more projects to complete for my American professors, but I could do those at my leisure. Once my classes ended during the second week of March, I planned on traveling throughout Europe for the next four months. But all the other study abroad students from my school were returning to the States, so I was on my own.

I had gotten very close to my host family during my stay in Germany, and shortly before I prepared to leave, they gave me a wonderful gift: they refunded all the money they'd received for my room and board and offered to let me stay with them anytime I wanted during my next four months of travel. With a lot more money than I had planned on, I took off on one of the biggest adventures I could've imagined.

Since I was now an expert in responsibility, I tried to do a lot of my travel at night. With the money from my generous German family, I was able to upgrade the four-month Eurorail pass I'd already purchased to first class for only a hundred dollars. This ensured good sleeping arrangements whenever I was traveling at night, and then I wouldn't have to pay for a hostel or hotel.

I did spend some nights in hostels, though. Depending on what country or city I was in, they were all different. Some were dormitory-style, which accommodated several people in one room with a common bathroom. Others were much smaller and only required me to share a room with one other person. Some of the places were every bit as nice as a hotel, and I would occasionally get my own room.

There were also times when I would hear about other places to stay. Early one morning as I was arriving in Oslo after a night of travel, I was walking out of the station alongside two American girls. A lady approached us and asked if we needed a place to stay. Her charge was equivalent to five US dollars a night. The three of us looked at each other, then at the lady, and without a second thought, we all agreed. When we got to her house, which was only one stop away on the bus, we were surprised to find we'd be sharing one small room with two sets of bunk beds. We quickly introduced ourselves since we hadn't met on the train. It just seemed like the proper thing to do; after all, we would be sleeping together that night.

A few days later I was in Amsterdam, witnessing things that would've made New Orleans blush. On my first night there, I stood in De Wallen—one of the most notorious red-light districts in the world—dipping my french fries in mayonnaise and watching customer after customer enter and exit the various storefronts. Each proprietor had her own space with a separate entrance, a huge picture window, and blinds that closed once a client entered. The rooms were sparsely furnished, usually with no more than a bed, a small table, and a chair. In that line of work, not much more is needed. But what really struck my curious young mind was the large, framed permits that were conspicuously displayed in each space. Someone told me later that it was all legal provided the prostitutes were checked frequently for STDs and kept their licenses up-to-date.

Pot was legal too. People were toking freely while strolling down the streets without a care in the world. I had only tried it on a few occasions at home, once with my stepsiblings and a couple of times with college friends. In those instances, it must've been substandard because it never did much, other than give me the munchies.

One night, I paid a few guilders for a cot on a tiny boat that was docked on one of the many canals. I had to share the intimate space with a young Indian guy, so we talked for a while before he asked if I wanted to try a hit of good hashish. Not wanting to appear uncool, I said, "Sure." A few hours and a lot of laughs and french fries later, we fell onto our cots, exhausted, stoned, and euphorically content.

While in Amsterdam, I also visited the Anne Frank house, saw Van Gogh originals, toured and sampled the beer at the Heineken brewery, and took a day trip to Keukenhof for the annual tulip festival. I returned each night to my uncomfortable little cot and my new best friend, Nikhil, and his stash.

After a few days, Nikhil and I hugged goodbye, and I left for the City of Lights. I arrived at six in the morning on a beautiful spring day. Leaving the train station, I found a café and stopped for coffee and a croissant. I struck up a conversation with a Frenchman seated at a nearby table, and he told me about a small hotel not far from there. It was in a perfect location, just blocks from the Arc de Triomphe, so I decided to investigate.

After checking in, I set out on foot to explore the city. That evening, I decided to go back to the same café. When I got there, I glanced around, wondering if I was in the wrong place because it seemed different. I even stepped outside and looked at the sign again to make sure. I was, indeed, at the right place, but the café had morphed into a nightclub. Something about it seemed odd, though. Two things, actually. First, only men were patronizing this nightclub—lots and lots of men. And second, no one was talking—at all. When the music stopped, there were no sounds other than the clinking of glasses. Then I realized that everyone was using sign language. I had found a gay, deaf bar, which couldn't have worked out better for me. Not only was I finally getting closer to accepting what I'd known about myself for a long time, but I also spoke no French. However, I soon found that I could communicate with gestures—my own form of sign language. It was a win-win for me, so I returned every night after that.

From Paris, I headed to Spain. My father's brother was stationed with the US Air Force in Zaragoza, so I stayed with him, my aunt, and my young cousin for a week. My aunt and uncle, bless their hearts, tried to fix me up with their daughter's babysitter, Alma, who was a cute, boyish girl. Even though we obviously didn't click, I had a lot of fun with her and Maria, her best friend, who insisted on being called Mario and made Alma look almost feminine.

After a week there, I was satiated with chorizo, olives, and sangria. I bid my uncle and his family goodbye and hopped on yet another train bound for Huelva, a coastal town on the Gulf of Cádiz in southwestern Spain. It was the perfect time of year, not too hot and not too cold. And even though Huelva could be touristy, it was the off-season, so I got a hotel room right on the beach for the equivalent of six US dollars a night.

While there, I planned to finish a couple of essays that had to be completed for my study abroad in Germany before I returned to the States. I paid the desk clerk for two weeks, thinking that would be plenty of time to finish. I didn't know a soul there, so I figured I wouldn't be tempted to do anything else—or so I thought. Destiny, fate, and kismet can, and often do, have a funny way of rearing their heads when we least expect it, and before I knew it, I was having the time of my life with my new Spanish friends. For the next two weeks, Jorge, Pablo, and I were inseparable—*los tres amigos*—going to soccer games, local clubs and hangouts, and spending countless hours smoking cigars and drinking *cervezas* as we discussed all the issues of our young lives. They laughed at my Mexican accent as they tried to teach me the Castilian pronunciations.

They cheered and whistled when I finally lisped, "*Sair-vay-thuh! Sair-vay-thuh!*"

I hated leaving, but after two weeks, I hadn't written a

single word for my essays, and I had to get them done. I said "*adios*" to my new friends and boarded a train to Heidelberg.

My German family was happy to see me, and it felt good to be back. For the next few days, I hunkered down in my room and feverishly worked on my projects. Lucky for me, when I'd arrived almost five months earlier, I had converted one of the drawers in the large antique wardrobe across from my bed into a treat shop. It was filled with all kinds of necessities: gummy bears, Nutella, an assortment of cookies, and foot-long Toblerone bars. The only time I left my room was at four o'clock every day for what they called *Kaffeestunde*, where the family gathered together for some coffee and whatever mouth-watering delicacy they had picked up from the bakery down the street. It was a ritual, and even though I was busy, it was important to have that time of fellowship—and eat a slice of cake or two.

A week later and twelve pounds heavier, I met my American friend Margaret at the Heidelberg train station. She was working as a nanny for a German family, and for several weeks, we'd been planning a trip to Greece. It was a long and grueling train ride to Athens—fifty-two hours to be exact—and my upgrade to first class didn't apply after we crossed into Yugoslavia, so we were forced to head back to the cattle cars. When we finally arrived in Athens, we found a small hotel to stay in for the night.

Our true odyssey began when we set off on our backpacking trip the next morning. It quickly dawned on us that people didn't backpack through Greece like they did in other places in Europe. We drew a lot of attention as we trudged through quiet little villages where tourists had obviously never been sighted before. We were even invited into a few homes, and although no one spoke English and the only expressions I knew in Greek were "My name is Dimitrios," "Thank you," and "Happy Easter," communication was never a problem.

One night, a large family invited us into their home for dinner. Afterward, as we sat sipping ouzo, the father suddenly stood up and smashed his plate on the floor. Then everyone else started smashing their plates. Margaret and I looked at each other, our eyes wide with surprise. Nevertheless, numbed by ouzo and encouraged by our new friends, we smashed our plates to smithereens too. *Opa!*

After two weeks in Greece, Margaret and I returned to Heidelberg. I stayed with my host family for a few more days before catching my flight back to the United States. Although I was exhilarated from my travels, I was ready to go home. Aside from the two weeks I'd spent there over Christmas break, I'd been gone for almost a year.

On my nine-hour flight to Detroit, I had a nice conversation with one of the flight attendants. He told me about his job in great detail, explaining the travel benefits, how schedules worked, the different home bases, and the rates of pay. He also said that speaking another language or two was a huge benefit when applying. It all sounded so glamorous.

I'd soon be starting my senior year of college, so in less than a year, I'd be graduating with a double major in German and Spanish. After that, I was toying with the idea of getting my master's degree in international business. If I did that, though, I knew I had to get serious and start applying to grad schools soon. But each time I gave it some serious thought, my mind wandered right back to becoming a flight attendant.

In early 1978, during the second semester of my senior year, I finally went with my heart and applied to the three largest airlines. Most US carriers had only begun hiring male flight attendants in the early 1970s, so it was still a bit of a novelty. By this point in time, less than 10 percent of flight attendants were male. Even so, I reasoned with myself that if it was meant to be, it would be.

And apparently, it was meant to be.

I was hired by not one but two of the major carriers. I went with my first choice and started my flying career in December 1978, a few months after graduating from college.

Initially, I only planned to do it for a couple of years. Then I would either go back to school or get a "real" job. But in no time at all, I'd hit my two-year mark. And although I'd already flown to a number of destinations, there were still so many more to see. So I decided to do it for one more year. But that turned into another, and then another.

Before I knew it, thirty-five years had passed in the blink of an eye. Those thirty-five years were filled with countless memories, most of which were wonderful. I've visited places even my wildest childhood dreams never took me to.

I've climbed the Great Wall of China, taken a boat to Estonia, basked in the beauty of the Taj Mahal, witnessed beautiful sunsets from atop the blackened cliffs of Santorini, had afternoon tea in London, smelled cherry blossoms in Japan, tossed coins into the Trevi Fountain in Rome, gotten rowdy with the locals at a pub in Dublin, meditated on a beach in Acapulco, been awestruck by the splendor of the Swiss Alps, taken a wine tour in Napa Valley, gone whale watching in Maui, eaten mussels in

Brussels, marveled at the brightly colored houses in Old San Juan, and peeked up kilts while listening to bagpipes in Glasgow.

It seems like a lifetime ago that a small boy spent hour after hour flipping through the pages of a world atlas, hoping that someday he'd be lucky enough to see those places. He has been lucky—very lucky—but he was also taught that with determination, perseverance, and hard work, *anything* is possible. And it all started with some crazy dreams.

Come Out,
Come Out

As a child and teenager, I was a bit of an oxymoron. At school and while in the company of others, I was the perfect student and friend, always well-mannered and cheerful. At home, however, I was often strong-willed, argumentative, bullheaded, and moody. "Don't sass me, young man!" and "Quit pouting!" were phrases I often heard.

After every parent-teacher conference, in which I was always given glowing reports, my poor mother would shake her head and ask, "Why can't you be like that at home?"

I was a good student, but I really had to work at it. I always got my homework done, studied hard for tests, and never once skipped a class. In my junior year, I was elected vice president of my school's National Honor Society. I graduated in the top ten percent of my class the following year and won the American Legion Good Citizenship Award.

I started college when I was seventeen. I attended a small, private liberal arts university where most of the students were there because of their brains and their family's wealth. I was there because I'd studied a lot, my family didn't have a lot of money, and I got a scholarship. Although the scholarship was generous, it wasn't a full ride, so to make up the difference, during my freshman year, I took a job with the university's food service department. I started out as a doughnut maker, getting up at four in the morning seven days a week. I'd always arrive at my first class of the day smelling like fried dough. Those seated closest to me would frequently say, "Mmm . . . you smell good! I get hungry just sitting next to you!"

As a reliable and efficient employee, I was soon given more hours, and before long, I also held the prestigious position of driving a catering van to all the sorority and fraternity houses every Friday and Saturday night. Now, when I say *catering*, I don't mean to imply that it was anything fancy. It wasn't like the attendees of the drunken sorority and fraternity parties would've even *appreciated* hors d'oeuvres and fine delicacies. Snack food was much more effective after a night of guzzling beer and smoking doobies, so food services came up with the bright moneymaking idea that the morning doughnut maker (me) could sprinkle all the leftover doughnuts and doughnut holes with powdered sugar, fill a couple of giant thermoses with lemonade (which I'm pretty certain were spiked within seconds after I delivered them), and haul those to the different frat and sorority houses. Since I couldn't afford to be in a fraternity (or sorority, for that matter), it was a fun job that gave me a bird's-eye view of all the sordid things that happened in those places. Not only did I witness wild parties but also hazing rituals, which included all kinds of crazy stunts and a lot of disgusting nudity. *God*, how I wanted to be in a fraternity!

In my senior year, I was ready to move on from my doughnut and lemonade tenure, so I got a job as a wine steward at a local dinner theater. I had fulfilled the requirements of my double major in German and Spanish the year before, so I was taking mostly fluff courses, which allowed me more time for my new career. The job required a vast knowledge of wines—something I did not possess. Oh, I knew a lot about my two *favorite* wines, but the dinner theater didn't even serve Boone's Farm Strawberry Hill or Mogen David's MD 20/20. So I had to start from scratch with Wine 101, learning everything there was to know about pinot noirs, cabernet sauvignons, rieslings, chardonnays, and ports.

The dinner theater had only been open for a few months when I started, so there really wasn't a curriculum for learning the different wines. The owner, John, simply gave me a menu to memorize and encouraged me to do wine tastings every night after closing. I've always been one to follow instructions well, especially from an employer, and to this day, I'm still not sure how my '67 Olds Cutlass and I found our way back to my apartment ten miles away every night. I just think it was a very smart car.

Although there were several other students working there, we never carpooled, probably because I had my extracurricular wine tasting obligations after my shift.

One night after work, as I was trying to focus on my eight glasses of wine, someone asked, "Mind if I join you?" It was one of the actors from the dinner theater. I hadn't met him yet, but I'd heard rumors that he was boinking the leading lady. It was a pretty professional group of actors, with several of them coming from Broadway and off-Broadway productions. I'll admit that I was a bit smitten that this good-looking, talented actor, who was also the dinner theater's musical director, wanted to join me. I was also very aware that he was heterosexual—unless, of course, Sarah, the leading lady, was actually a man in drag. Heck, they were actors, so I figured anything was possible.

"I'm Andrew," he said as he took the seat across from me.

We sat and talked for a long time while I did my wine homework. He went to the bar and opened a bottle of Mouton Cadet bordeaux, his favorite, and gave me a glass. I considered this extra credit and wondered if I was becoming a wine snob who no longer gravitated toward Boone's Farm or Mogen David.

Andrew and I had a nice generic conversation and found that our hometowns weren't that far apart. He was about ten years older than me and had worked with several of the other actors before. They all lived in their own small loft apartments above the dinner theater while they were doing this show. The current production, *The Fantasticks*, was about to end, and rehearsals for *Caberet*, which would include several new cast members, were starting the following week. I casually asked if Sarah, the leading lady, would be playing Sally Bowles.

"No, she's going back to New York," Andrew answered. I feigned my sincerest disappointment when I heard this.

My twenty-first birthday landed two weeks after I met Andrew. I had a full day of classes that day, then worked at the dinner theater until almost ten thirty. Just as I was finishing my shift,

Andrew approached me and put his hand on my shoulder. "Hey, Jim, the girls are having a party tonight. Wanna go?" By "the girls" he meant Jeannie and Susan, two lesbians I'd met a couple of times. They were the first openly gay couple I'd ever known, and I wasn't exactly comfortable with that whole scene. True, I had dipped my toes in the gay waters a time or two (okay . . . maybe six times!), but I had pulled them out quickly. I was still trying to convince myself that I really wasn't "one of those people," so I considered those six times as nothing more than experimentations on my journey to hell. However, because it was my birthday and I didn't have other plans, I agreed to go.

"Great!" Andrew said. "It's just a couple of blocks from here. Let me know when you're ready to go."

The girls' apartment was in an old building in the downtown area of this small midwestern town. When we arrived, we made our way up the three flights of stairs to their apartment. As we got closer, the sound of rowdy laughter became louder and louder. Once inside, I realized the source of the racket was Terry, one of the *extremely* flamboyant actors. How flamboyant was he, you ask? Let's just say that he made Paul Lynde look butch.

"Happy Birthday, girlfriend!" he screamed, planting a big wet kiss on my cheek. I was absolutely mortified because up until that point in my life, I could count on one hand—two fingers, actually—how many times I'd encountered someone like Terry. One time was in junior high and the other was in high school, and both guys had been cruelly taunted and made fun of. I, too, had been called "sissy" and "queer" on several occasions, but I worked hard to make my bullies think otherwise. In fact, during my freshman and sophomore years, I even played on the football team. I hated football, but it seemed like the right smoke screen at the time. To this day, I know very little about the game, but I did perfect my peripheral vision in the locker room.

Anyway, had it not been for the fact that Andrew was by my side, I probably would've run right back down the stairs and skipped the party. But he *was* there, and he *had* invited me, and because he no doubt was *very* lonely since Sarah, his leading lady, had returned to New York, I decided to stay.

From that point on, the rest of the night remains somewhat fuzzy. I do remember having fun, though—lots and *lots* of fun! And I do remember drinking scotch to get rid of my nervousness—lots and *lots* of scotch. But I soon got sick—very, *very* sick. Or so I was later told.

The one thing I do remember clearly is waking up on the bathroom floor around six the next morning, smelling of scotch and vomit. I looked around, wondering where I was. That's when I realized I wasn't alone on the floor. Andrew was right there with his arms wrapped tightly around me, sound asleep. When I stirred, he squeezed me gently, and in that romantic moment of scotch, vomit, toilet paper, and lust, I felt my heart surge. As I dipped my toes into the gay waters this time, unlike the previous times, I let them dangle for just a bit longer and then linger before slowly and fully immersing them. Then, after a while, I very slowly and reluctantly pulled them out, more satisfied than I had ever known possible.

In the days that followed, I constantly worried about being found out. I wondered if my coworkers at the dinner theater, who'd also become my friends, would turn their backs on me if the word got out. Word did get out, but they didn't turn their backs on me. On the contrary, they became somewhat protective of me and never mentioned it to any of our mutual acquaintances on campus. Everything was blissfully sweet until the night Annie Aronson came to see a show at the dinner theater.

I'd met Annie in a ceramics class the previous semester. Within minutes of meeting her, seconds perhaps, I knew her entire life story. She made no qualms about the fact that her father was a very wealthy businessman and that she was engaged to a guy named Hugh, who had graduated the summer before and also came from megabucks. Annie, who belonged to one of the sororities on campus, was the type of person I neither liked nor disliked. Her looks were the same—she wasn't butt-ugly nor was she drop-dead gorgeous. She was, however, *very* impressed with herself—especially the night she arrived at the dinner theater with Hugh.

After the show ended and my duties were completed, I went to the bar to see Andrew. To my dismay, he was sitting with Annie and Hugh. When he saw me, he beckoned me over to their table.

"Jim, this is Annie and Hugh," he said, making the introductions, unaware that Annie and I knew each other.

Annie smiled insincerely and said, "I almost didn't recognize you, Jim, all handsome in your tux and bow tie and *not* smelling like a doughnut."

Hugh shook my hand halfheartedly as he scanned the room for better company—or an empty table. The place was full, so he returned his full attention to the snifter of Courvoisier XO Imperial on the table in front of him.

The next hour and a half was extremely painful for me because the conversation centered around three things: Annie, Hugh, and money. Being an expert on relationships since mine with Andrew was well into its third week, I couldn't help but notice how unhappy this engaged couple seemed. Annie was constantly trying to get Hugh's attention, but the more she tried, the more sullen and disinterested he became. At the end of the evening and her fifth glass of wine, Annie was hanging over the table, grabbing both Andrew's and my hands. I guess this was her desperate, drunken attempt to make Hugh jealous.

About a month later, as I was waiting to cross a street on my way to class, a silver Camaro Z-28 glided to a stop next to me. As the power window opened, Annie popped her head out. "Hey, you! Like the car? It's Hugh's, but he let me borrow it."

"Very cool," I said, wondering what she'd think of my old clunker.

"I was going to call and ask you a favor." I waited, not quite sure what I could possibly do for her. "My sorority's fall formal is a week from Saturday, and that turd Hugh is going golfing in Florida with a buddy. It's not like he can't go some other time, but he won't bend, even though I already got the tickets."

Golfing in Florida was starting to sound good to me too, even though I had never golfed—unless miniature golfing counts.

"Would you go with me?" Annie asked as she revved the engine ever so slightly. "I'll have his car."

I felt a bit trapped, so I told her I'd have to check with my boss because weekends were always busy at the dinner theater. In reality, I wanted to ask Andrew how I could get out of it. After all, he was an actor and ten years older than me, so I figured he had a lot more experience with situations like this than I did.

I was wrong. When I told him, he started laughing and said, "Go with her! I think it'll be fun! It's a free night out, and you'll get to rub elbows with all the rich sorority girls. Go!"

It wasn't the *elbow* rubbing that was worrying me, and even though my gut was telling me to come up with a good white lie for an excuse, I took Andrew's advice and called Annie the next day to tell her I would go.

"That's great! And just so you know, I made reservations at the same Hyatt where the dance will be."

"Oh, I . . . uh . . . I thought we were coming back that night."

She laughed then said, "Who's going to want to drive after partying?"

"Yeah, I guess you're right. So how much do I owe you for my room?" I asked innocently.

"I told you, the whole thing is my treat. Besides, I'm not going to let you pay me for *sharing* a room."

At that point, I was *really* getting nervous.

"I'll pick you up at three on Saturday," she said and hung up.

By Saturday, I was actually sick to my stomach from worry, which Andrew found quite amusing. "Just relax," he said. "She's not going to try anything. She's engaged, remember?"

He's right, I thought. After reassuring myself that Annie was happily engaged to Hugh, I relaxed a bit, knowing I really had nothing to worry about. I spent the rest of the afternoon running errands, packing a small overnight bag, then waiting for Annie to pick me up.

She arrived right on time, and soon we were cruising along the expressway to Lansing, some sixty miles away. Once we arrived, we checked in and unpacked the car. The room, which was beautifully decorated, was much nicer than any of the hotels

I'd ever stayed in before, including the Marriott in New Orleans. But rather than having two double beds, this room only had one king-size bed. I started getting nervous again.

Annie must have sensed it because she quickly removed a gift bag from her suitcase and handed it to me. "Here. This is for you."

The first thing I pulled out of the bag was a box of Fannie Mae chocolates. *Now we're talkin'*, I thought to myself. Next was a small bottle of Chivas Regal scotch, which I knew was pretty expensive. *Silly me, spending all this time worrying about nothing. Maybe Annie isn't so bad after all.*

After that, I retrieved a bottle of Halston cologne, which was also not cheap. I smiled at Annie as I reached into the bag again, this time feeling something soft. I felt again, looking at her questioningly as she smiled back at me. I couldn't help but notice how pencil-thin her lips were—quite a contrast from her redwood-sized legs. I reached into the bag again, my fingers tracing the soft material until they found an elastic waistband. My curiosity got the best of me, so I quickly pulled out the item. When I saw what it was, I immediately shoved it back into the bag.

"Don't you want to try them on, silly?" Annie asked. By "them" she was referring to the new Jockey underwear she'd gotten me. "Come on . . . they're bikini briefs. I bet you'd look great in them."

"Uh . . . no thanks," I muttered, not quite sure what else to say.

"Then let's have a drink." She didn't sound happy, and I noticed that her thin lips had disappeared altogether.

I went in search of an ice machine and brought a bucket of ice back to the room. As I opened the door, she quickly closed and latched her suitcase, turned to face me, and pointed toward the table where she'd set up a bar with bottles of gin, tonic, and the Chivas Regal from my gift bag. I made us each a drink and held up my glass to her.

"Thanks," I acknowledged.

"For what?" she wanted to know.

"Well, for asking me to come to this. And for all the gifts."

"Oh, I haven't given you *everything* . . . not yet anyway," she smiled seductively, her lips suddenly reappearing.

We both took a drink from our glasses.

"You know my roommate, Nancy?" Annie asked out of the blue.

I did. She had also been in our ceramics class and was in the same sorority as Annie. She wasn't in Lansing, though, because she hadn't been lucky enough to land a date for the formal.

"Well, she said she thinks you and Andrew are . . . you know . . . ," she remarked as she waved her wrist at me a couple of times.

"Huh?" I wasn't liking where this was going. I felt my face turning a lovely shade of crimson, so I took a big gulp of scotch. "What do you mean?"

"You know . . . you and Andrew. She thinks you're . . ." This time her limp wrist action was even more exaggerated.

Oh God! I thought, then emptied my glass.

"But I told her you aren't, and I said I could prove it."

At some point after my third glass of Chivas Regal, I asked what time dinner was starting.

"Six o'clock," Annie replied as she stretched out on the bed. "But we really don't have to be there right then. They'll serve cocktails first, then dinner at seven." After a momentary pause, she kicked off her shoes and continued, "We don't even have to go if you don't want to."

"Uh . . . no. We'd better go," I tried not to slur, "since you already have the tickets and all."

She opened her mouth to argue, but I was already on my way to the bathroom to shower. I grabbed my toiletry kit and gift bag, balancing them both with my fourth drink as I pulled the door shut with my foot.

Once I made sure the door was securely locked, I started rummaging through my new bag of goodies. I sprayed a little Halston on my wrist and snarfed down a chocolate. I took a quick shower, then used my leaf-blower-sized Conair to style my coif. Once every hair was in place and lacquered down, I noticed my new undies at the bottom of the bag. Before I could rationally think of the consequences, I pulled them on, admired myself in the mirror for a moment, then opened the door and started prancing around the room.

Annie sat on the bed, smiling and motioning for me to come closer. This caused my common sense to momentarily return, and I stopped mid-gyrate and went back to the bathroom to get dressed. I put on my shirt, then reached under my suit coat to retrieve the pants from the hanger. But I came out empty-handed. There were no pants!

I ran back into the main room and told Annie I couldn't find my pants. She could've cared less. "I guess we'll just have to stay here then," she cooed as she stretched out fully on the bed and patted the spot next to her.

Over the course of many years, I've replayed that scene in my mind over and over again. And I always end up asking myself the same question: *What the HELL were you thinking, strutting around in those tiny bikini briefs like that?* I honestly don't know if I did it to tease her or, if on some level, I was just trying to prove a point. The only point I did prove for certain was that scotch—four glasses to be exact—makes me very, *very* tired.

The next thing I knew, it was morning. I painfully opened one eye and realized I was still wearing my dress shirt and bikini briefs. *Where am I?* I wondered. I felt a sense of déjà vu because, just weeks before, something similar had happened at Jeannie and Susan's apartment. However, this time, I didn't wake up with strong, manly arms holding me.

I slowly opened the other eye and allowed the dimly lit room to come into focus. *Okay,* I started to remember, *last night I was here in this hotel room with Annie, and we'd been drinking. I took a shower, and while I was getting dressed, I realized I didn't have any pants. Then Annie said it was okay, that we didn't have to go to the dance, then she patted the bed next to her and . . . Oh no. OH NO!* I screamed inside my head. *Had I caved in and done the nasty with her? And if so, what was it like? Did she enjoy it? Did I enjoy it? Had I used protection? Or would a little Jimmy or little Annie be making his or her debut in nine months? And how could I have pulled it off since I didn't find her even remotely attractive? Had I just liked the feel of it?*

I carefully turned over to see if she was even there. She was—in all her thin-lipped glory—sitting with her back against the headboard, arms crossed tightly, wearing nothing but a black teddy!

"Good morning," I croaked.

"What's so good about it?" she spat.

Clearly, she's pissed off, so it must not have been good for her. Maybe I hadn't found her G-spot, I thought. *Not surprising since I just heard the term for the first time on the* Phil Donahue Show *a few days ago. But more importantly, I hope she wasn't expecting a do-over.*

"Let's get out of here," she grumbled as she got up and headed to the bathroom.

The hour-long drive home was—for lack of a better term—quiet. There was no discussion of whether we'd be having a boy or a girl, how we'd rocked each other's worlds the night before, or how much we loved one other. None of that was mentioned because not *one single word* was uttered.

When I got back to my off-campus apartment, I called my mom, whom I hadn't spoken to for a couple of weeks. She asked how the dance had been, which really surprised me since I hadn't told her about it.

"Oh, didn't Annie tell you?" Mom replied. "Your brother and I met her on Tuesday."

"You *what*?"

"Yes, she was here on Tuesday. She said she was in the area, so she decided to drop in to meet us. Scott really loved her car. She even took him for a ride! So how long have you two been dating?"

Dating? I thought. *We aren't—nor have we ever been—dating. What is Annie up to? She had to do some big-time planning to just "drop in."* My mom and brother still lived in my hometown, which was two hours from campus, so Annie couldn't just drop in, especially on a school night. Plus, she'd told my brother the car was hers. Something wasn't adding up.

The next day, I couldn't stop thinking about the fateful formal night. I dissected everything in my mind over and over until I suddenly remembered something: When I'd gone out for a bucket of ice, I seemed to have surprised Annie when I came back into the room. I didn't have a key, so she was probably expecting a knock on the door when I returned. But I hadn't shut the door all the way, so when I returned, I just walked in. That's when I saw her hurriedly close and latch her suitcase like she was trying to hide something. I couldn't help but wonder if my missing pants had somehow found a new home in her suitcase. The likelihood of them just falling off the hanger was almost as nonexistent as her lips were when she was mad. *She must've set this whole thing up,* I concluded. *Without my pants, we couldn't go to the dinner-dance, so we were forced to stay in the room, which was exactly what she wanted. But, in the end, I guess I showed her.*

At least I thought I did until a few days later when I received a letter from a longtime friend from home who was also a college classmate. The letter went something like this:

Dear Jim,
I thought we were much better friends, but obviously I was mistaken. I just found out from Sandy who found out from Kathy who heard from Brenda who heard from Annie Aronson that you're a homosexual. I just can't believe it, Jim. Why didn't you tell me? I thought we were friends, but now I realize I never really even knew you.

At that moment, a terror I had never known gripped me so tightly I could barely breathe. I'd just been outed by a miserable, fat-assed, no-lipped, sexually deprived, two-faced, teddy-wearing sorority bitch. What frightened me the most, though, wasn't the fact that everyone at our small college probably knew my secret by now. My biggest fear was that my family and friends at home would soon know too. Annie would make sure of that.

But I was *not* going to let her win this one.

The following morning, I phoned my boss at the dinner theater and told him I had an emergency at home and wouldn't be able to work that weekend. I packed up my car and went home with one purpose in mind: I was going to tell my family I was gay, starting with my mother. I was more afraid of telling her than anyone else, probably because I was most afraid that she'd be upset and reject me.

Once the surprise of seeing me wore off, Mom and I had a nice dinner with my brother, then caught up on everything. Well, almost everything. Each time I was on the verge of bringing up the subject, I'd lose my nerve. Finally, as we were saying good night, I sat down on her bed and blurted it out. I'll never forget my tender words: "Mom, I'm a queer!" A *queer*—that's exactly how I put it. That was the word I'd often heard while growing up, and I knew her generation used it too. Using that term left absolutely no room for misunderstanding.

I'll also never forget her response. Her face softened as she said, "All I've ever wanted is for my kids to be happy. Are you happy?"

"Yes," I responded as I finally found the courage to look at her, "happier than I've ever been."

"Then I'm happy too." She smiled as she put her arms around me.

We stayed up all night talking. For the first time, she opened up about her divorce from my father. She said that, although they loved each other very much, they were just too young and immature to try to work things out.

We talked about all our similarities, which were endless. She shared with me how she, too, had been stubborn and bullheaded just like her own father was. The two of them had butted heads throughout her childhood and teenage years, but in later years, they'd become very close.

"It wasn't easy," she admitted. "And even though he was the same way, he was always trying to change me. Now I realize that I tried to do the very same thing to you, even though I wanted to spare you from all that."

The conversation eventually turned to my confession earlier that night. "Mom, did you ever suspect that I was . . . you know . . . different? I mean, I was never into sports, except when I played football—and that was a complete ruse. I hated it. But didn't you find it strange that I always loved helping you and Grammy with the cooking and cleaning? I wasn't exactly your typical boy."

"No, but that's what makes you special to me," she continued with a smile. "You're not the norm. You were always so sensitive. I was always aware of that, even when you were acting out your emotions—anger, frustration, or whatever."

That was a defining moment for both of us. We now understood so many things neither of us had even tried to understand before. My parents' divorce had affected me tremendously, and hiding who I really was had been detrimental in more ways than I had ever realized.

But I no longer had to hide.

Thanks indirectly—or directly—to Annie Aronson, something wonderful happened that night: my mother and I stepped away from our roles as mother and child, perhaps for the first time in our lives. Until then, our very similarities had often been our greatest challenges. But after I came out to her, those similarities and differences melded into one, and at that moment, she became the friend I needed more than anything else in the world. For that, I will always be grateful to all the teachers in this journey called life, including Annie Aronson. They not only helped me recognize, embrace, and nurture my own self-love and happiness, they also gave me the courage to be strong, yet sensitive, to always live in the moment, to believe in myself, to strive to never judge, to praise others often, to open my mind and heart to all possibilities, to let go of anger, to forgive quickly, and to love unconditionally.

It took twenty-one years, but with immense gratitude, I finally accepted who I was meant to be.

A Smile or
a Smirk?

"Smile and the whole world smiles with you." Whoever coined that phrase was obviously trying to write a hit Broadway show. And chances are, he or she had never been a flight attendant.

As a child, I recall my mother telling me that her dream had always been to be a stewardess. But in the early 1950s, there were two necessary requirements for this once-glamorous profession: the applicant must be female with a minimum height of five feet two. My mother, who was definitely female, was barely five feet tall. She needed a stepladder to kick a duck in the ass. This put the kibosh on her flying career, so she quickly accepted her first runner-up dream of becoming a mother to three screaming brats by the time she was twenty-six.

There were two reasons for the height requirement. First, a stewardess was expected to be tall, poised, and beautiful—not unlike a fashion model. The second reason was more practical: Part of the job description required a stewardess to hoist mammoth-sized bags onto the overhead racks, the predecessor of today's enclosed overhead bins. And she had to be tall enough to do this in a professional, ladylike manner—in high heels, no less. Heaven forbid she'd ever have to stretch upward, possibly exposing her girdle-clad derriere to the aft portion of a full DC-7. No, she was expected to do this with a courteous, effortless flair and a smile plastered on her heavily made-up face at all times.

During my last semester of college, I sent résumés all over the country. All over the world, actually. Being a language major, I felt I'd be a huge asset to whoever was lucky enough to hire me. Once word got out that I had graduated and was looking for work, I figured companies would probably be begging me to come on board.

"You speak English, Spanish, *and* German? We'd be truly honored to have you, but how can we ever afford a genius like you?"

I knew the possibilities were endless.

I could be hired as a top-ranking executive with an international company, wining and dining clients all over the world. The fact that I knew nothing about the products they sold wouldn't be an issue once the clients heard me order our meals in German, Spanish, and English.

Or maybe I could simply become one of the greatest teachers of all time. After all, I had just finished my student teaching at a local high school, and I was more popular than my host teacher, Señor Rheinhardt. Of course, that wasn't saying much. He was one of the most boring teachers I had ever experienced and often put his whole class to sleep, including me.

Restaurant work was also an option. After all, I'd worked in the food service department for three out of my four years of college, and I knew that big cities were home to some of the finest German and Spanish restaurants in the country.

The biggest challenge would be deciding which job to take once the calls started pouring in. However, that proved not to be such a challenge after all because my telephone never rang. Dejected and a bit irritated at the world for not recognizing the magnitude of my talents, I strolled over to the Career Placement Office a few weeks before graduation. The bulletin boards were plastered with notices for teaching positions as well as the business cards of various headhunters who were too lazy to actually go out and scout around for potential candidates. As I breezed over these, a small flyer caught my eye:

INTERESTED IN A HIGH-FLYING CAREER?

Have you always dreamed of being paid to travel?
New York on Monday, Acapulco on Tuesday,
Toronto on Wednesday.

Do you love working with the public?

¿Habla español?

Call for an interview.
800-LUV-2FLY

For my first interview, I was flown to Dallas in first class and offered champagne and canapés. I was starting to like this job very, *very* much. The flight attendants were extremely gracious, and after they heard I was going for an interview, they shared some pointers: "Say this . . . ; Don't say that . . . ; Smile . . . *always* smile! Oh, and remember, you *love* people."

Once I arrived at headquarters, I was shuffled into a large room with twenty-five other grinning fools. We smiled at one another but were too nervous to speak. Our interviewer, Rodney, entered the room and immediately put us at ease. As he explained every aspect of the job—from the good to the bad to the downright ugly—I soon realized that the airline industry had changed a lot in the past twenty-five years. Stewardesses, or flight attendants as they were now called, no longer had to wear girdles. And it wasn't mandatory for them to wear eyeliner and six-inch-tall come-fuck-me pumps, for which, I presume, the majority of male flight attendants were grateful. But one thing hadn't changed: flight attendants were still required to smile at all times while in uniform. From the time we left our humble abodes to the time we crawled into bed at the end of a long and grueling three-day trip from hell, we had to have those smiles plastered on our faces.

Not surprisingly, with my stellar qualifications, I got the job. My initial training, which lasted six weeks, took place at a facility in Fort Worth, Texas, that was affectionately known as the "Charm Farm." Of course, I knew nothing of this nickname until those of us lucky enough to graduate were out "on the line." I was just so excited to be among the small percentage chosen for this prestigious job. It was like winning the lottery.

Among the sixty-five people in my training class, only eight had penises—that I know of. Being a flight attendant was still primarily a female job, which made us males stand out even more in class. That's precisely what we did *not* want to do.

From the time my fellow penis bearers and I arrived at the Charm Farm, so eager to please, we were scrutinized by big-haired instructors with names like Betty Ann, Jo Ann, George Ann, Sue Ann, and Tim Ann. They watched every move we made as we shuffled to and from classes in food preparation to passenger care to emergency procedures.

As the weeks progressed, so did the weeding-out process. Fellow classmates could mysteriously disappear at any given moment. We would return from a bathroom break and *poof*, three more would be gone. Maybe they hadn't smiled while grunting in the bathroom stall. It was all very unnerving.

During the last half of training, we attended grooming classes. There were hairstylists, poised and eager to cut, color, and—I use this term loosely—style those who were crazy enough to come to training with long and beautiful hair. They walked in looking like Cher and left looking like Little Orphan Annie. It was scary.

We also had to attend classes on the application of makeup. The instructors were still a little unsure of what to do with those of us with penises, so someone had the bright idea to teach us to apply bronzer, while the girls were made up to look like flying hookers. I think I would've preferred the latter. Hour after hour, we applied streak-free bronzer and learned the virtues of hairspray. I'm sure it was quite an experience for the straight male flight attendants. We left the grooming room looking like Little Richard, with hair twice the size of our female counterparts.

Manicure class was next. The girls spent hours pushing their cuticles and filing and painting their talons, while we were taught to simply push back our cuticles and buff our nails.

"You can never buff enough," George Ann would say.

As I had in college, I took my classes very seriously. I wanted to get it just right. Over time, I learned to push back my cuticles to the first knuckle and then buff my nails to a luster that forced people to shield their eyes. And through it all, I smiled like an idiot.

On graduation day, we looked like the Stepford flight attendants. *We* couldn't even tell ourselves apart. While talking with a classmate, you had this eerie feeling you were looking in a mirror.

It was also a day of great pride. We'd made it through this aviation boot camp. We had adhered to a new set of rules—rules that would remain with a lot of us for the rest of our lives. But, in a way, it was also a day of liberation because we could finally fart for the first time in six weeks.

We couldn't contain our excitement as we anticipated the next phase of our lives: moving to new cities, making new friends, and our new looks. It was a complete makeover, airline-style.

Still smiling, we hugged each other at the end of the ceremony, shortly before being whisked off to the airport where we'd all board flights to various cities that we'd soon call home. My new home was called Dallas. My new supervisor was called Barbara Ann.

The next morning when I reported to Barbara Ann, she smiled and said, "Hi, darlin' . . . how y'all doin'? I love your hair." Then she told me which flights she'd accompany me on to check my work performance, explaining that she would be grading me on three different phases of the flight: the boarding process, the meal service, and passenger interaction.

"Now, after the meal service, I want you to converse with each and every passenger on that airplane—and at all times with a smile. Do you understand?"

"Oh yes, ma'am. And by the way, I love your hair too," I lied through my fake smile.

I've had that same smile plastered on my face for over forty years now. I've smiled so much I've pulled muscles in my face. I've smiled through the threats of belligerent passengers who wanted the beef we just ran out of. I've smiled as passengers have foamed at the mouth over seating assignments. I've smiled as children spewed their SpaghettiOs all over me. I've smiled while being propositioned by the wine-guzzling woman in 4J whose husband just went to the bathroom. I've smiled as I threw out three vertebrae while trying to lift a little old lady's hundred-pound carry-on bag into the overhead bin. I've smiled when I realized that I'd been up for twenty-seven hours. I've smiled when a four-hundred-pound man said, "I don't feel so good" just before landing on top of me as he passed out. I've smiled upon realizing that the couple in 16A and 16B are *not* sleeping under the blanket they're sharing. I've smiled as the captain announced, "We seem to have a hydraulic leak and will have to make an emergency landing in Iceland." I've even tried to smile through tears as a young wife told me that the body of her husband, who was killed in an automobile accident, is in the cargo area below. I've smiled reassuringly as two hundred people nervously watched my reaction to severe turbulence at thirty-five thousand feet. I've smiled through my own personal crises, simply because it felt better to smile than to curl up into a little ball.

All these years later, I'll probably keep on smiling. It just seems easier to do so in hopes that the whole world, or at least a part of it, will smile right back.

In Tune

I tossed and turned for a while before finally rolling over and looking at the clock. It was 8:45 a.m. I pulled the covers back over my head. I wanted to go back to sleep, but I couldn't. I was wide awake. It was my thirtieth birthday, and I wasn't at all happy about it. Grammy Long always said that change becomes more difficult as we age, but being the exception to most rules, I wasn't crazy about it when I was young either. And I was officially no longer young.

It really wasn't so much about turning another year older that bothered me. It was about leaving one decade and stepping into another. *I'm in my thirties, for God's sake! I've just barely figured out how to make my twenties work.*

The night before, I'd decided I would deal with this the only way I knew would work for me—by *not* dealing with it. I would simply sleep the day away, giving me the escape I needed. I just wanted to be alone. Or at least that was my plan. That soon changed, however, when the sound of the doorbell brought me back to reality, which is exactly where I did not want to be.

At first I tried to ignore it, but it was becoming more and more apparent that whoever was pushing the button was not going to stop until I answered. So I grudgingly stumbled out of bed and threw on some clothes as I ran down the stairs.

Before I even got there, I could see my next-door neighbor through the window. As I fumbled with the lock, he started to yell, "Those damn morons who put up your privacy fence sunk one of the posts right next to my garage!"

When I finally got the door open, I was face-to-red-face with him. "They must've been using a sledgehammer because all the shit I had on the top shelf in the garage vibrated right off and fell on that old toilet I was going to use in the half bathroom."

"You mean that old gray Kohler that's been out there for years?" I asked, wondering why he wasn't actually thanking me for finally putting it out of its misery.

"Yeah, well, it's actually white . . . or it would've been once I cleaned it up. I just haven't had time to put it in yet. Anyway, those bastards broke the tank cover, and I know it's irreplaceable because it's so old. I'm sure it's an antique and probably worth a lot of money."

I was quite certain it wasn't a *valuable* antique. Oh, I'm sure it had probably had its fair share of asses perched on it over the years, but the broken piece could've most likely been replaced for a couple bucks.

"Can it be glued?" I questioned.

"*Glued?* Hell, they smashed it to smithereens! There's no gluing that crumbled pile of porcelain. I bet it'll cost at least twenty-five bucks to replace it."

I doubted it would cost that much but decided just to give him the twenty-five dollars.

As he was leaving, check in hand, he turned and said, "And I want that goddamn fence moved away from my garage by tomorrow afternoon."

My thirtieth birthday was not starting off well. I considered going back to bed, but I was too upset. An adult temper tantrum is an ugly thing to witness first thing in the morning. Maybe I should've played on his sympathy and told him it was my birthday, although I doubt it would've worked.

I started a pot of coffee, and as it was brewing, I reflected on my life so far. *I guess I do have a lot to be thankful for: a good career, a great partner, a supportive family, and a house that I love.*

I shuffled to the bathroom and studied myself in the mirror. I turned on the light and moved in for a closer look. Scrunching and contorting my face, I examined the lines around my eyes.

"You inherited your laugh lines from me," my father had told me a thousand times. "Not wrinkles—those are *definitely* not wrinkles—they're laugh lines! You can thank my side of the family for those youthful genes."

Just then the phone rang. Speak of the devil. "Happy Birthday, Junior!"

Being called "Junior"—although this moniker was saved for special occasions, like birthdays—was something I loathed. I wished I could find a way to tell my dad how much I hated it.

"Thanks, Senior," I replied with a touch of sarcasm.

"Huh . . . *wha* . . . oh . . . ha ha."

I had finally found a way.

"I was just sittin' here wonderin' how my kids had gotten older than me. Any idea how that could've happened?" he laughed.

Before I was able to answer, he continued. "Guess who I ran into at Kmart last week. Remember Hop Copenhaver, our old neighbor on Johnson Street? Had one leg shorter than the other? Anyway, we got to talkin', and he asked about you kids, so I showed him our family picture from Olan Mills, you know, the one we had taken back in '83. Well, he just couldn't believe it . . . said you and I looked more like brothers than, well, you know . . . what we *are*."

"You mean father and son?"

"Huh? Oh yeah. Hey, did I tell you your stepmom and I won the dance contest at the Elks Lodge last Friday night? They said they'd never seen anyone jitterbug like we did. They thought we were too young to even know what it was!" he chuckled.

"Uh . . . yeah, you mentioned that when you called to tell me your doctor said you had the prostate of a twenty-five-year-old."

"A twenty-*one*-year-old," he corrected. "Have you had yours checked yet? If you do, you really should schedule a colonoscopy too. You could probably have both done at the same time. Maybe get a two-for-one deal. They're kind of accessible through . . . well, you know . . . the same place. My doctor said it's never too early to start that. You're thirty now, remember?"

"Yeah, I remember," I grumbled.

"Well, I'd better get back to work. No rest for me since I'm just too young to even think about retiring. But I wanted to wish my old man of a son a happy birthday. Maybe I'll see you at the health club tonight. Oh, did I tell you I weighed a hundred forty-five at the doctor's office when I had my physical? He told me to keep doin' what I'm doin'. What do you weigh now?"

"I'm not sure. My scale is broken," I fibbed, even though I hated lying to my father.

"I'll let you borrow mine. Your weight always has fluctuated a lot, hasn't it? Well, happy birthday!"

I was beginning to question my earlier decision to be alone all day. Perhaps I needed the company of good friends. Jack Daniels, Jim Beam, and the Walker men—Johnnie and Hiram—came to mind.

When the phone rang again, I reluctantly picked it up. "Hello?"

"Do you know what I was doing thirty years ago right now?"

"Hi, Mom."

I heard her take a long drag from her Winston.

"Going through the longest labor anyone has ever endured. It was hell. Did I ever tell you how you got stuck right there in the birth canal? That idiot doctor just left you there, half in, half out."

"That must've hurt."

"Hurt? *Hurt?* Imagine pushing an eight-and-a-half-pound ham through a nostril and then have it get stuck! That's why you have that ridge on your forehead."

Suddenly, her tone became reflective. "Actually, it didn't hurt all that much since they had me so doped up. Thank God for drugs. I must've been hallucinating, though, because I thought I heard you screaming, 'Get me out of here!' Later, the nurse said it was *me* screaming, 'Get it out of there!' Damn, those were some good drugs."

"Sorry about that," I said, rubbing the ridge on my forehead.

"But it was all worth it," she laughed. "Of course, I didn't realize it until you were about twenty-eight or so."

"And why's that, Mom?" I asked, sensing my cue.

"Because you were one of the meanest brats I've ever seen. A little shit. You're damn lucky you lived beyond your fifth birthday. There were times I could've killed you."

"I'm glad you didn't," I laughed.

"Jesus, you were a rotten kid. I used to wonder where you got such a mean streak."

"Must've been Dad's side."

"Oh, speaking of your father, I saw him and your stepmom at Kmart a few nights ago. I got to hear all about how they'd won some damn dance contest. He never took *me* dancing. No, I was too busy changing shitty diapers and wiping dirty handprints off the walls. *Dancing?* Hell, the only time I danced was with a mop."

I looked at the clock and wondered if nine thirty in the morning was too early for a cocktail.

She continued, "Anyway, as I was leaving the store, I heard someone yell, 'Hello there, beautiful.' I hurried and looked around the checkout lanes and remembered I was in Kmart, for God's sake—*Kmart*—where the term *beautiful* is rarely, if ever, used. Then I saw our old neighbor Hop Copenhaver, and I swear he undressed me right there with his eyes. Always was kind of a pervert. I used to see him hopping all over the neighborhood, making eyes at just about everyone. Remember how he used to give you kids candy? I'm surprised he ever snagged Marie, but she was no prize either. Anyway, he said he'd just seen your father—probably heard all about the dance contest too. I guess your dad showed him a picture of you kids because he went on and on about how I couldn't *possibly* have a thirty-year-old son. He almost tripped over his good leg when I said my daughter was two years older. He said I looked more like your younger sister than your mother. Can you believe that?"

My youthful genes were suddenly feeling very, very old.

"It made my day, that's for sure. Even if it came from a short-legged pervert. Let's see now, if my big brother is thirty, I couldn't be more than twenty-eight or twenty-nine," she laughed.

When our conversation ended, I looked at the clock. It was only quarter to ten. Maybe I did need to get out of the house for a while. But everyone I knew—my partner, Rich, all of our friends, and even my new "younger siblings," whom I had once referred to as "Mom and Dad"—was at work that day. *If I decide to do anything today, I'll be doing it alone. But that's what I wanted all along, isn't it?*

I went upstairs and took a shower, and just before I left the house, I called Rich at work. "Wanna break away and have lunch with me?" I asked.

"I can't. We've got a meeting at eleven thirty, and I don't know how long it's going to last. Besides, you told me you *wanted* to be alone."

"Oh, I know . . . and I *do*," I lied. "That's okay. I'll see you later anyway."

"Don't forget . . . we've got reservations at Murphy's tonight," he said. "And that really good piano player is supposed to be there. You know, the one who can do just about anything: show tunes, classical, jazz, whatever. I'd kill to play like that."

My first stop I remember well. The Emporium, an upscale bistro, was in the downtown area. It sat on a small hill overlooking the river. Two sides of the restaurant were all windows, which afforded patrons a beautiful view of the swiftly moving water below. It seemed a befitting place to be—on my birthday especially—because I could sit sipping a martini, letting my thoughts drift right down the river. I'd never had a martini before, but it just seemed like the right thing to do.

I arrived just before eleven and had to wait a few minutes for the doors to open. After they did, I was led to a small table in the corner, where the two glass walls met, and ordered a martini. I took my first sip, trying not to make a face from the taste. Other people—*beautiful* people—were now filtering in. They sat, nursing their own cocktails, lunching on fancy salads and sandwiches served on huge croissants with decorative lettuce. My second sip went down more easily, and by the third, my dark cloud was lifting. The soft music, exquisite view, and alcohol seemed to be the perfect blend. Within minutes, my glass was empty, and my outlook was considerably brighter. I ordered another drink and then another. I believe I even had a fourth, but I don't recall. Whether I even had lunch that day remains a mystery.

The next thing I remember clearly was sitting in my kitchen with a payment booklet in my hand. I studied the cover, wondering what it was. My bank's logo was on the front, and as I opened it, a sense of dread slowly washed over me. I looked down and noticed a bill lying on the table. Picking it up, I felt the blood drain completely from my face as reality sank in. After just sixty easy payments, I would be the proud owner of a shiny black baby grand piano!

A piano? I bought a piano? We can't afford a piano! I berated myself. *We're barely squeaking by with the mortgage and car payments. And what'll I tell Rich, especially since I just ripped him a new one for not using a twenty-five-cent coupon for a box of Cheerios?*

"Twenty-five cents saved is twenty-five cents earned," I'd scolded him.

My mind went into overdrive as I tried to figure out what to do. *Maybe I can hide it from him until I come up with a really good explanation. But how do I hide something the size of a hippopotamus?*

Camouflage it behind a bunch of houseplants? Throw some black paint on the walls and hope it blends in?

Hiding it from Rich and wondering how we were going to pay for it weren't my only concerns. *What caused me to make such a huge and impulsive purchase in the first place? Depression? Alcohol? Have I just suffered my first midlife crisis? I could maybe understand buying a new car, but a piano?*

True, Rich had learned to play as a child and had often said he would love to have one someday "when we can afford it." And I'd never made a secret of my own childhood dream of becoming a great concert pianist and singer—a young Liberace of sorts. Over the years, however, reality had put a damper on those dreams. The likelihood of me ever becoming a famous piano player was growing slimmer and slimmer, especially since I'd never even taken a lesson. *Maybe I can change all that now. After all, writing out a check for the monthly payment could light a fire under my butt.*

Besides, it wasn't as if I was a *complete* stranger to music. I actually made my musical debut in the fourth grade. My partner was a flutophone, a small red-and-white plastic instrument, not unlike what the Pied Piper might've carried as he meandered through the streets of Hamelin, followed by all the children. The Pied Piper's musical abilities probably surpassed mine, however.

Anyone in my fourth-grade class who was willing to pay the two dollars received the flutophone and lessons. The idea behind it was to weed out those who had absolutely no ear for music. Knowing this certainly didn't include me, I begged my parents for a flutophone, and even though my mother thought it was a waste of money, my father finally relented.

"But Dad, I'm the only one in my whole school, the whole town, and *probably* the whole state of Michigan whose parents are divorced. Can I puhleeeeze have a flutophone?"

Worked like a charm.

By the following week, several of us had signed up to meet for daily flutophone practice. Our music teacher, Miss Pamela, was a mousy little waif of a woman who rarely showed any sign of emotion. However, at our first practice, she professed her love for both music and her flutophone. She suddenly became a well-spring of emotion.

"Hello students! My name is Miss Pamela. As in Pame-la-la-LA—notice how musical it sounds?" she trilled. With that, she broke into a tune which, thank God, I've never heard repeated. As she lovingly caressed her worn flutophone, she sang *a cappella*:

I love to go a-wandering,
With flutophone in my hand.
And as I go, I love to play,
That's why I don't need a man.
Pamelee, Pamelaa, Pameleeee,
Pamela-la-la-la-la-la,
Pamelee, I'm PameLA,
That's why I don't need a man!

Then she lifted the flutophone to her quivering lips, and with the toe of her no-nonsense shoe tapping, she belted out the same tune sans lyrics. By the end of her performance, we were *all* exhausted.

She brushed away some loose wisps of hair that had escaped from her tightly bound bun, pushed her thick glasses back to the top of her nose, and smiled contentedly, "I hope someday you will all love your flutophones half as much as I love mine."

As the weeks progressed, I did develop a sort of liking for my flutophone. I wouldn't exactly call it love, but it did cooperate as I learned new notes and simple tunes.

With the holidays fast approaching, Miss Pamela-la-la was hell-bent on teaching us a handful of Christmas songs. One day she entered the room, breathless. At first we thought she'd been playing with her flutophone, but she soon shared her excitement. "The county home for the elderly has asked *us* to perform! Can you believe it?"

We couldn't. But it was great inspiration for us to learn new songs. We practiced and practiced, anxiously awaiting the big day. When it finally arrived, we loaded up our flutophones and caravanned, along with our proud parents, to the local old folks' home. Upon entering, a reporter approached us and said he was doing a piece for the local paper—a story about us!

Unfortunately, our excitement promptly turned to disappointment when we learned that because of either a recent flu epidemic or a bad prune pudding at lunch that day, the old codgers couldn't come down to the community room to watch us perform. But the facility's director had a solution. "Why don't we have you play your songs over the public-address system?" he enthusiastically suggested. "We'll just have you stand around this microphone. That way even the hard of hearing can enjoy it."

Enjoy it? Obviously, he hadn't heard us play yet.

We surrounded the mic and waited for Miss Pamela-la-la's lead. On cue, we lifted our flutophones and started to play. It was magical to hear our music—along with the crackling static of the antiquated PA system—permeate the halls. But above it all, we could hear the residents' comments.

"What the hell is that racket?"

"Turn that thing off!"

"My father's iron lung had a better beat."

"Clara just threw her hearing aid out the window!"

"Is that the fire alarm?"

The reporter was somewhat kinder when he printed his review the next day. Some of the highlights were: "You've never heard anything like it!" "Two generations in perfect harmony." "'Jingle Bells' brought down the house!" "Every toe was tapping, every finger snapping!" "A day we'll always remember!"

By fifth grade, I was ready to move on. Unlike Miss Pamela-la-la, I felt I'd reached the end of the road with my flutophone. Besides, it had served its purpose. It either whetted our appetites for music or sent us scurrying in the opposite direction. Some were musically inclined, others were not. I was beginning to realize that I fell into the not-so-musically-inclined category, but I wasn't about to give up.

One day after lunch, the entire fifth grade class was led into the gymnasium where band instruments had been set up for our inspection. The smell of spaghetti, green beans, and cling peaches still lingered in the large room.

There were no pianos, so I gravitated toward the saxophone, my second dream instrument. I picked it up, in awe of its brassy beauty. A lady approached and instructed me on how to first wet the reed.

"Wet it *real* good, honey. Really saturate it."

I salivated like I'd never salivated before.

"Now blow," she said.

I did exactly as I was told, but for the life of me, I could not make a sound. I blew and blew, but nothing came out. I blew so hard I farted, but that was the only sound I emitted—and it was off-key.

"Well, I see you're not a sax sort of guy, young man."

I was crushed.

"Why don't you try another instrument?" she suggested in a flippant tone.

I grudgingly walked to the next instrument in line and picked it up, thinking, *But I don't* want *to play the trumpet!*

Just then, a guy with long hair walked up to me and said, "Hey, man, you like that horn?"

"I dunno," I mumbled, unable to fake my disinterest.

"That little guy can be your friend, man."

I needed a friend.

"Whoa, man! You've got some big ole honkin' lips—too big for *that* horn," he laughed. "But go ahead and try to blow anyway."

Again, I blew and I blew. The only thing I heard that time was my ears popping. I still hadn't found a friend.

I continued my journey to the snare drum, but by this time, I was ready to pound the holy hell right out of it—which is exactly what I did. I was soon informed that even snare drums have feelings and should never be hit so hard.

I looked around and realized that the only remaining instrument was the trombone, which was sitting alone in the corner. It appeared to need a friend too, so I moved in its direction.

"Perfect. *Absolutely* perfect!"

I blinked as I looked around for the source of this praise. Then my eyes landed on a man with the largest lips I'd ever seen. He was staring right at me.

"Maestro!" he cried out. "I've found the perfect mate for this trombone."

What the heck is he talking about? I wondered.

"You've got the perfect lips! Want to attach them to my friend here?"

I hesitantly moved forward.

"Pucker those big lips, my friend, and put them right here on this mouthpiece. You're about to experience heaven on earth."

I followed his directions to a tee and let loose. I'm pretty sure I almost blew the gymnasium away.

"Wow!" he exclaimed, fanning himself as he regained his footing. "That was *incredible!*"

At the end of the day, we were sent home with the recommendations from the "experts," who were nothing more than salespeople from a local band instrument company.

"Like hell I'm buying you a saxophone!" screamed my mother. "And wait a minute . . . it doesn't even *say* saxophone here on this form. It says trombone."

Oh well. It was worth a try.

"A trombone?" Mom grew pensive. "Your Uncle Sonny has an old trombone. He's the only one in our family who was even *remotely* musically gifted. I bet he'd let you use it."

I soon met my new friend—a dilapidated, rusty, old vagabond of a trombone whose case could've passed as a steamer trunk had it been smaller.

How will I ever carry this thing on the school bus? I wondered where my uncle had received this treasure, especially since he was the first in our family to show any sort of musical ability. Maybe my grandparents had lost a bet years earlier and this was the booby prize.

The trombone I could handle—and even the camper-sized case it resided in. But the sawed-off plunger used for a mute was unacceptable. There was still dried toilet paper on it!

This quickly became a bargaining tool with my mother, and shortly thereafter, an agreement was reached. I would learn to play—or attempt to do so—this once magnificent instrument, if she would pay the three dollars for a new mute.

It was a deal from hell.

Every day for the next few years, I hauled my new friend home. I rarely practiced, but I must say, it was the cleanest trombone you'd ever want to meet. It spent hours soaking in the bathtub. I've always been a bit anal retentive, so I was constantly worried about the cleanliness of my spit valve. And, at the risk of being dubbed a braggart, I had the cleanest slide for miles.

In sixth grade, a friend of ours came to my mother with a proposition. "The Golden Agers club members would love to hear the kids play. Kind of a band concert, I guess."

By "the kids," she meant her daughters, Candy and Linda, me, and a kid we'd befriended only because he was good on the drums. Candy was a natural on the clarinet, and Linda left me in the dust on her trumpet. Mike, the drummer, was prone to sinus infections, but when he wasn't blowing his nose, he could really hold his own. Then, there was me.

We practiced and practiced, and when the day of the concert arrived, unlike the flutophone performance at the old folks' home, we had a good view of our audience.

I'll never forget the distorted looks on their faces, their fingers in their ears, and the toothless sneers as they grimaced and begged for mercy. I should've thrown in the towel on my music career right then and there, but I didn't. Instead, much to the dismay and disappointment of all who knew me, I was more determined than ever to learn.

Not only did I continue soaking my trombone in the bathtub, I even started practicing once in a while. It didn't take long for me to learn that the blaring—which sounded like a cow giving birth—drove our miniature poodle, Pepe, absolutely bonkers. Whenever I belted out a note or two, his eyes would actually turn scarlet red, like he was possessed. Sometimes, for fun, he would attach himself to the end of the slide, just above the spit valve, and dangle there while growling viciously as I carried him around the house to the tune of "Lemon Tree." My repertoire never included much more than that and a handful of other simple tunes because, despite all my years of junior high and high school band, I usually faked it, which was easy to do since I sat between two gifted, yet nerd-ish, trombone players who always drowned me out. Sometimes—no *usually*—when I didn't know a song, I'd simply puff out my cheeks and act like I was blowing. Even if I couldn't play, I certainly put on a good show. And being in the school band got me out of having to take phys ed.

And now, many years later, I sat in the kitchen I shared with Rich, holding a payment booklet for something we couldn't afford. I needed to fabricate a story—and fast. According to the paperwork, the piano was scheduled to be delivered the following day. But as hard as I tried, the scheming, plotting, and conniving side of my brain wasn't cooperating. Perhaps it was still soaked in gin from the three—or was it four?—martinis. Whatever the reason, I was at a loss. *How am I going to tell Rich?*

Dinner at Murphy's that evening was outstanding, despite the fact that I never shut up. Between bites, I nervously rambled on and on, talking about any and every unimportant thing imaginable. I knew it was a stall tactic, but I couldn't find the words to tell him about the piano. I wanted to enjoy the evening—especially since I knew we wouldn't be able to afford to eat out again for a long, long time.

After we finished the meal, we ordered a couple of brandies. A few minutes later, as we sat sipping them, listening to the music coming from the Steinway in the corner, I knew the time had come. The setting and the ambience were perfect, so I cleared my throat and tried to sound casual. "Oh, by the way, I bought a baby grand piano today. It's being delivered tomorrow morning." I yawned and nonchalantly picked up my snifter.

"You bought a *what?*"

"A piano," I replied, looking around for the nearest exit.

"You bought a *piano?*" he asked, wide-eyed.

"Uh, yeah."

"Oh my God! You know I've always wanted a piano! That's great!"

This wasn't the reaction I'd anticipated.

"What kind is it?" Rich asked enthusiastically.

"Uh, . . . it's a Zimmermann . . . made in Germany. It's one of the few baby grands that has a solid wood soundboard." I had absolutely no idea what that meant, but I'd read it in the brochure, and it seemed like the right thing to say at the moment.

Rich couldn't conceal his excitement. We chugged our drinks and quickly paid the bill. Then we rushed home and spent the next couple hours rearranging the living room in anticipation of our new arrival.

Within a week, the piano seemed comfortable in its new surroundings. And within a month, it felt like it had always been part of our family. Despite my earlier concerns, we didn't have to take out a second mortgage to pay for it. On the contrary, it got us through some of our leanest years, saving us a lot of money on entertainment. Many evenings we ate dinner at home then relaxed in the living room, with me snuggling on the sofa with our pooch, Maxi, while Rich happily tickled the ivories. The soft piano music and a roaring fire will always remain one of my favorite memories.

Over three decades have passed since I bought the piano. It still resides in our living room, in all its black sleekness, boasting that it has a solid wood soundboard. I've taken many piano lessons over the years, yet, to this day, I can barely pound out the simplest of tunes. The reason seems clear: I've never found the right teacher.

Or perhaps I have. Maybe I'm both the student and the teacher in my *own* life. Maybe we all are if we open our minds to that possibility. Besides, it's not really about learning to read and play someone else's music; it's more about living and loving to the fullest, all the time fine-tuning and harmonizing the relationships we hold most dear.

It's taken me a long time to realize—or rather accept—this, but now that I have, I feel like a master musician in the concert of my own life.

Liberace would be proud!

Mean Old
Queen

It was the summer of 1993, and we had just boarded our flight to Frankfurt when the captain made his first announcement. "Good evening, ladies and gentlemen. Welcome aboard. *Guten Abend, meine Damen und Herren. Willkommen an Bord. Buenos tardes, señoras y señores. Bienvenidos a bordo. Bonsoir, mesdames et messieurs. Bienvenue à bord.*"

Who the hell does he think he is? The lead in Cabaret?

"Well, ladies and gentlemen, I'm Captain Gary Haggerty, and I'll be in command of this magnificent aircraft tonight. I'm also in charge of a group of lovely flight attendants in the back. Well, Jim isn't exactly my idea of lovely, but he makes a mean hot fudge sundae—for those of you lucky enough to be in first class."

I instantly decided who *wasn't* getting one of my mean hot fudge sundaes.

"Anyway, I've got some good news and some bad news . . ."

The cabin immediately fell silent.

"Well, the good news is that we still serve food on these international flights, even for you folks in . . . economy." He almost whispered the term *economy*, as if it were a dirty word that he was embarrassed to say in mixed company.

"And now for the bad news. Are you ready?" He paused momentarily, presumably for dramatic effect. "We've just been informed that we'll have a little delay here in Chicago."

The passengers let out a collective sigh.

"Seems we have a pesky little hydraulic leak," Captain Gary chuckled. "Don't you just *hate* when that happens?"

I looked around the cabin as the passengers listened intently. Unlike the captain, they didn't see the humor in it.

"Not to worry, though, *meine Damen und Herren*, we have the best mechanics in the business working on it right now—in their long underwear, no less. As most of you know, it's colder than a witch's you-know-what here in Chicago, and those poor guys are not superhuman. They get cold too—so cold that they have to come inside every few minutes to avoid freezing anything off.

"I've always said our mechanics are amazing. What they can do to a jet engine truly humbles me. It makes me very, *very* proud to be the captain *and* commander in chief of this ship—a ship that'll be fixed quickly and efficiently, I can assure you."

Does he realize he's on an airplane and not the Starship Enterprise?

Captain Gary continued. "Now, just sit back, relax, and press your passenger call buttons should you have *any* concerns about the connections you might not make once we get to Frankfurt. My very professional flight attendants will be happy to assist you."

Ding! Ding! Ding! The sound was deafening. You could barely hear the mechanics revving up the jet engines outside the windows. Had there not been two air marshals seated between me and the cockpit, I would've personally run up and put the captain out of his—and our—misery.

Ding! Ding! Ding!

As fingers frantically searched for call buttons, my own hands began to tremble as I pictured myself wrapping them around Captain Gary's deeply tanned neck. I fantasized squeezing until I saw his lips curl back in a pleading grimace, exposing his perfectly capped white teeth—which I was quite certain were not covered by our dental plan.

Smiling at this vision, I realized my anger didn't stem from the fact that he had just told the truth to a plane full of people. Nor was it because he had taken ownership of an entire 767 crew by saying, "*my* very professional flight attendants will be happy to assist you."

I wasn't even mad that he'd shared with two hundred passengers that I make a mean hot fudge sundae for those lucky enough to be seated in first class. I wasn't even working in first class that night—I was way back in steerage, where a hot fudge sundae is nothing more than a Dairy Queen memory.

No, the reason that I wanted to strangle Captain Gary with the cord of the microphone from which he'd just given his speech was that I, a "qualified German speaker," now had to translate everything he'd just said. And by the questioning looks the passengers were giving one another, it appeared that the majority of them spoke very little English. They seemed to only understand key phrases in the captain's announcement, like "delay here in Chicago," "hydraulic leak," "press your call buttons," "hot fudge sundaes," and "connections you might not make."

I quickly picked up the microphone and translated—sort of.

"Ladies and gentlemen, my name is Jim, and along with eight other very professional flight attendants, we're here for one important reason: *your* safety. Our primary concern is to get you to your destination in a safe and timely manner. However, our best mechanics are working on a small mechanical problem right now. I've been assured that they can fix it and will get us on our way shortly. The agents in Frankfurt are all very aware of your connecting flight situations and will be there to assist you upon our arrival.

"Oh, and by the way, due to our delay, all the ice cream on board will have melted by the time we take off, so regrettably, there will be no hot fudge sundaes today, even for those of you seated in first class."

Ding! Ding! Ding!

Much to my dismay, the chimes did not let up. In fact, they were like the rapid-fire shots from a machine gun. *DING! DING! DING! DING! DING! DING! DING! DING! DING!*

I looked above the passengers' seats, expecting to see a dozen or more call lights illuminated. However, there was only one, above seat 11H.

DING! DING! DING! DING! DING!

I raced up the aisle, expecting a crisis situation. Perhaps someone was dying. "Yes, sir," I panted, finally reaching row eleven. "Is there an emergency?"

"Well, it took you long enough to get here," the young man occupying 11H admonished as he rolled his eyes.

Long *enough? I ran down the aisle so fast I could've qualified for the Olympics!*

"Do you need something?" I asked, still out of breath.

"Need? *Need?* Did you just ask me if I need something? Does it look like I need something?"

A more natural hair color and a personal trainer, I thought. But I hesitated to voice my opinion because I didn't want to upset him further. *A passenger complaint on the same day I strangle the captain might not look good on my permanent record.*

"I *need* something to drink."

I sprinted to the nearest galley, retrieved a glass of water, and returned to 11H as fast as possible. "Here you go, sir."

"What the *hell* is this?" he spat. "Did I say I needed *water?* Did you not hear me?"

People inside the terminal could've heard you.

"I *NEED* a cocktail!" he barked.

So do I! I thought to myself, but my professionalism, although tested, would not allow me to actually say that. "I'm sorry, sir, but we're not allowed to unlock our liquor carts until after take-off." Then I hightailed it away from him.

DING! DING! DING!

"Yes, did you want some more water?" I asked politely, realizing that my patience and professionalism were waning—and not necessarily in that order.

"I WANT TEQUILA!" he bellowed.

"But we don't have tequila, sir. And even if we did, I couldn't serve it to you until after takeoff when we unlock our beverage carts," I reiterated with a smile.

Just then, the captain's voice came over the loudspeaker again. "Well, ladies and gents, looks like our awesome mechanics have taken care of that little problem. We should be taking off in about five minutes."

That was music to my ears.

DING! DING! DING! DING! DING!

That was *not* music to my ears.

"Yes, master—I mean mister—you rang?"

"I'm a member of your frequent-flier program . . . and well, somewhat well known in my hairdressing profession, and I have to say I'm quite appalled that I wasn't upgraded to first class. I trust that you can do something about it. I'm not at all comfortable sitting back here."

I studied him for a moment. "May I see your frequent-flier membership card?"

"Uh . . . well . . . I don't have it yet," he sputtered.

"Yet?"

"I just signed up at the ticket counter."

"Oh, so you're new to our program?"

"Yes, and the lady who signed me up said to ask the stewardess to be upgraded."

"Flight attendant."

"Huh?"

"We're called flight attendants . . . since 1970."

"Well, whatever. Now, about my upgrade—"

I would've happily moved him to first class just to get rid of him. But there was no way I was about to reward his rude behavior. Plus, I was starting to have fun. "Well, sir, we're not allowed to upgrade anyone on board. That's the agent's responsibility. Quite frankly, I'm surprised she told you we do it. Do you remember her name?"

"Hell no, I don't remember her name! I'm just telling you what she told me!" he hollered. Then he suddenly smiled, although it didn't quite reach his eyes. "Oh, I bet you could bend the rules just a *little* bit, couldn't you?" His smile inched up to the dark circles beneath his eyes, which he'd made a futile attempt to conceal.

He leaned out into the aisle and gestured with his head toward the first-class cabin. "I can see an empty seat up there . . . right next to that tall, muscular man."

"Sorry, but that seat is reserved for the pilots. It's their rest seat, and it's nonnegotiable. It's a contractual thing."

He glared at me.

"Just like those seats right there," I said, motioning a few rows back. "Those are the rest seats for the flight attendants."

He turned to see where I was pointing.

"Right back there . . . the ones with the footrests and curtains. It's kind of hard to see them with all those first-class pillows and duvets piled on top of them. Anyway, passengers are not permitted to sit there either."

His smile took a sabbatical.

"Well, we're about to leave. I'd better take my jump seat. Oh, and would you please fasten your seat belt?"

Just then, I spotted a large bag under the feet of the couple in 10H and 10J. They obviously didn't seem to mind having their knees to their chins, but this was a safety violation, so I said, "Sir, we need to get that in an overhead bin before takeoff."

It took all three of us—the man, the woman, and me—to wrestle the heavy, oversized bag into the bin above their seats, which, by the grace of God, was empty.

As I made it to my jump seat seconds before we rolled down the runway, I thought to myself, *Do they have a family member inside that bag?*

Shortly after takeoff, as we were making our steep climb to thirty-five thousand feet, a passenger pressed the call button. Without even looking for the source, I made my way uphill to 11H.

"Long time no see," I said as I leaned over to reset the light.

"Soooo . . . we've taken off. . . . Where's my cocktail?"

This is going to be a long flight. "It's on the way, sir."

"And like . . . how long are we talking?"

"Well, like, as long as it takes to get the beverage cart set up and the airplane leveled off."

"I need some peanuts."

This guy needs more than peanuts. "We'll bring some pretzels with the drinks."

"What? Are you shitting me? You don't have *peanuts* anymore?"

"No, sir. We just have pretzels."

"That really sucks. I'll tell you one thing . . . you damn well better have my special meal."

I retrieved the passenger list from the nearby galley and searched for his seat number. "Are you Mr. Minoquin?" By the look on his face, my pronunciation of MEAN-oh-kween was incorrect.

"That's Mean-oh-kwahhhhh," he sniffed, sounding like a conceited duck.

"Oh, okay, Mr. MEAN-oh-kween. I'm sorry, but we don't have a special meal listed for you. What did you order?"

"A seafood platter."

"A *seafood* platter? That's strange." I forced a puzzled, yet concerned, look. "We haven't served those for several years."

"Oh, wait a minute. . . . It was actually a fruit platter."

"Hmm . . . that's another one we no longer serve."

"Then just give me a damn cocktail!"

"Right away, Mr. MEAN-oh-kween."

"Oh-KWAHHH!" he quacked.

Throughout the flight, I'm quite certain he developed a blister on his finger from pressing the call button so often. I was also pretty sure this was his first international flight or perhaps even his first flight ever.

"What? You charge for drinks? When did that start? I fly *all* the time, and they've always been complimentary. This is absolutely ridiculous! Seven dollars for a drink? Dis*GUST*ing!"

"We started charging a few years ago," I said as I handed him a bag of pretzels. "Have you not flown in a while?"

"Well, I . . . ," he stammered. "Oh, just give me a Maker's Mark and Diet Dr. Pepper."

I've got a real seasoned drinker on my hands. "I'm sorry, sir. We don't have Maker's Mark or Diet Dr. Pepper. How about a Jack and Diet Coke?"

"I bet you have Maker's Mark up in first class, don't you?" he purred.

"We do, but I see a first-class passenger drinking it, and we must have it available for him . . . seeing how much more he paid for his ticket and all."

"Then just give me a Jack Daniels and Diet Coke!" he snapped.

"My pleasure. That'll be seven dollars, please."

A lady who spoke only German was sitting directly behind the Mean Old Queen. So when I asked her what she wanted to drink in her native tongue, he turned around, obviously surprised that an idiot like me was able to speak another language.

I only look stupid, I wanted to say, but I kept my thoughts to myself.

On my next trip down the aisle, he asked for a "*vin blanc*," assuming I'd have no idea what he was talking about. I handed him a split of French white wine.

"*Merci beaucoup.*" He was obviously more impressed with himself than I was.

"*De rien*," I answered.

"Huh?"

"Oh, that means 'you're welcome' . . . *en français.*"

"Oh . . . yeah, right."

During the meal service that followed, we enjoyed a few minutes of peace and quiet. Mr. Minoquin, although not dining on a seafood platter or a fruit plate, ate every morsel of chicken, mashed potatoes, and carrots on his plate. Assumedly, he was getting over the fact that he had to pay for alcoholic beverages, considering the amount he was putting away.

Once we finished the meal service, I sat for a while in one of the flight attendant rest seats. At the end of my break, as I was coming out of the curtained area, a colleague approached me and said, "That nasty guy in 11H has had *way* too much to drink. You're going to have to cut him off."

Me? Why do I have to do the dirty work?

DING!

Oh great, I haven't even had a chance to brush my teeth before a new confrontation, I thought as I walked to seat 11H. "Yes, Mr. MEAN-oh-kween, what can I do for you?"

"Duh, what does it look like you can do for me?"

Several ideas crossed my mind.

"I need a grasshopper."

"Uh, we don't have grasshoppers."

"Then a Baileys and Coke."

"Well, actually, Mr. MEAN-oh-kween, considering how much you've already had to drink, I think it would be a good idea to slow down for a while."

"*Excuse me?*" He glared at me through bloodshot eyes. "Slow down? What the *hell* is that supposed to mean?"

"It means that we're going to have to cut you off for the time being. Maybe you can have a Coke or a cup of coffee—or take a little nap. Then later we can renegotiate whether you can have another alcoholic beverage."

"I *need* another drink!" he hissed, spraying me with spittle. "And you know why?"

Before I could even give him a smart-ass comeback, he smirked and let out a sinister chuckle as he slowly reached down and pulled his shirttail out of his trousers. I watched, somewhat bemused, wondering what he was about to show me. For effect, I yawned and looked around the cabin, seemingly bored. He slowly lifted his shirt up to his neck, exposing his large, dimpled belly.

"Because this hurts like a motherfucker," he growled.

As I searched for the exact source of his motherfucking pain, I wondered, *Is he referring to the deep stretch marks that start at his armpits and snake their way around his ample man boobs? Or could it be the shiny, obviously new tattoo on his chest? What a spurt of creativity he must've had when he decided to substitute the boring little arrow on the classic male symbol with a much longer and thicker phallic version.*

"Uh, yes, . . . I can see why you're in such pain," I sympathized.

"Well, that's why I *need* another drink!" he shouted. "For the goddamn pain!" It was becoming clear that he was even ruder drunk than he was sober.

"Sorry, sir, but I can't give you any more alcohol."

He stared at me for several seconds, possibly even minutes—I don't recall. Finally, stone-faced and with one eyebrow raised, he said, "Fine, then I'll just have to take some more Valium and Vicodin."

"I don't think that's a very good idea to be mixing those with alcohol," I said as I continued looking at him.

He suddenly smiled and sweetly asked, "May I have a couple bags of pretzels and an ice water then?"

"Certainly," I answered as I turned toward the galley, perplexed by the sudden change.

When I returned, I put the water and pretzels on his tray table. Without raising his eyes from the copy of *GQ* he was holding, he slowly raised his hand . . . well, actually, it was just his middle finger. As he rubbed the side of his nose closest to me with the finger, he smiled, still not looking at me, and said, "Thank you."

Not quite sure I was processing this correctly, I said, "Excuse me?"

Again, the middle finger rose and pointed toward the ceiling as he moved it up and down the side of his nose.

"I said, 'Thank you.'"

I leaned in close and whispered, "The negotiations are over. No more alcohol for you."

He ignored me as he continued reading about men's fashion. I was not harboring good thoughts of Mr. Minoquin at that moment, and as I turned to leave his row, I became a firm believer that negative thoughts can create negative events because I suddenly heard a strange sound. I looked back just in time to see the overhead bin above his seat fly open. At that point, the whole scene went into slow motion as the Winnebago masquerading as a carry-on bag miraculously unwedged itself and started falling toward my archnemesis's head. With lightning speed and the strength of Hercules, I caught the bag just before it made contact and hoisted it back into the overhead bin. Several people applauded.

"Boy, that was a close call," I said to him.

"*Close?* You could've *killed* me! Maybe if you had done your job and made *sure* the compartment was locked, that wouldn't have happened. You're pitiful."

I walked away, shaking my head.

A few rows back, a woman stopped me and said, "Wow! He could've been seriously injured! . . . You might've even saved his life." When she cocked her head, I'm sure she was thinking, *And you did this* why?

After we landed and deplaned, I was making my way through customs when I spotted Mr. Minoquin arguing with a customs agent. "What do you mean I have to show my damn passport again?"

I smiled and moved toward the line leading to the customs inspectors, grateful to be done with Mr. Minoquin and his shenanigans. As I approached a tall, big-boned man in a green uniform, I said in German, "Excuse me, do you see that gentleman over there? The one who's shouting?"

"*Ja*," the inspector replied curtly. His face remained expressionless as his eyes cut to Mr. Minoquin.

"Well, on the airplane, he was boasting about all the drugs he was carrying. And he insinuated that he was hiding them where *no one* could find them."

The inspector's eyes narrowed to slits as he reached for his latex gloves. "Really? *Danke schoen*," he said as he walked away while slipping the gloves over his grotesquely large, sausage-like fingers.

As I exited the customs area, I heard a loud commotion behind me. I turned just in time to see Mr. Minoquin being led to a curtained area.

I couldn't help but smile as I stepped outside into the cool morning air. The universe was about to balance itself out once again. True, I had finagled with it a bit, knowing that justice—in the form of an unexpected and complimentary rectal exam—would soon prevail.

It was going to be a great day.

Lest Ye Judge

In the fall of 1994, I was on the tail end of what had been a pretty quiet flight back from Milan. Well, it was relatively quiet until I sat down for my half-hour rest break. That's when a couple seated in the last row of first class, which was just on the other side of the flimsy partition in front of my rest seat, decided to have a discussion—a very loud discussion.

"You know, this relationship has always been about you and only you!"

"About *me*? What do you mean it's all about me? Why do you try to hurt me by saying things like that? I can't believe you sometimes. I've given you the best years of my life. And you say it's all about *me*? Do you even realize how hard I work to stay beautiful? And I do it all for *you*, not *me*! Do you have any idea how much time I spend having my hair and nails done? And do you honestly think I've had all those surgeries for *myself*? Yes, it's true that I like having a tight tummy and ass, and yes, I love the attention my big tits bring, but puhleeze . . . all about me? *I don't think so!* And don't forget—I gave up my career for this marriage!"

"*Career?* What career? You were a telemarketer when I met you!"

"I was in sales! And I was moving up the ladder. But then I met you, and you *forced* me to quit!"

"*Forced* you? You gave me an ultimatum! You said you'd only marry me if you didn't have to work."

"Well, being a wife—a wife who always looks *damn* good—is a full-time job in itself. Do you realize how many hours I have to spend with my personal trainer? And trust me, two massages a week can be *very* painful. I could barely get out of bed the morning we left on this trip. And that's another thing . . . all we ever do is travel. Travel, travel, travel! Acapulco, the South of France, Martha's Vineyard, Fiji, the Greek Islands. Have you ever stopped to consider *why* I'm so exhausted? If not for a week at the spa every three months, I honestly don't know how I'd do it. As it is, I can barely muster the energy to watch over the staff—which reminds me—you need to have a talk with the housekeeper. I found a dust ball on my treadmill last week and thought, *Oh my God! What if the people from the magazine had spotted it the day they were here doing the photo shoot! I would've died right there on the spot!* Oh, and the cook has been super stingy with the white truffles lately. What am I paying him for? Yet *you* have the audacity to say this relationship is all about *me?*" Then she hissed, "And where is that damn stewardess? I need another drink! You've upset me so much that I need another drink! And remind me to call my therapist when we get home. Thanks to you, he certainly has his work cut out for him! *All about me! ME?* How dare you make such an accusation, especially since you of all people know how much I've been through. It's no wonder I'm so fragile. Being in this state, I'm even apprehensive about going under the knife for my augmentation next week. If I die on the operating table, it'll serve you right. *All about me? I AM SO SURE!*"

Sitting in my rest seat, listening to her monologue, I had an uncontrollable urge to peek out from behind the closed curtain. Call me nosy, but I wanted to see this woman. *Rather nondescript,* I thought to myself as I watched her down the last of her chardonnay.

For the last few minutes of my rest break, I reflected on everything I'd just heard and counted my blessings for my own relationship and life.

"*All about me?*" she muttered. "What a *selfish* thing to say!"

I could tell this was a marriage made in heaven.

Since I knew I wouldn't be getting much rest on this break, I decided to get up. As I was strolling to the back of the airplane, a couple stopped me and asked for a customs form. I found one and brought it back to them. They seemed nice, so we exchanged a few pleasantries. As it turned out, they lived only a couple of miles from me and had been visiting friends in Italy.

"How long have you been doing this?" the wife asked.

"Almost seventeen years," I answered.

"You must really like it. How often do you make this trip?" .

"Once or twice a week."

"Isn't it difficult to juggle everything . . . this *plus* a family?" she eyed me quizzically.

Uh-oh. Without going into my own personal "stuff," I simply said, "Oh, a lot of people do it very successfully."

This answer didn't seem to appease her because she continued prodding, "Well, aren't you married?"

Here we go, I thought. "No, I'm not married," I stated simply.

She shook her head and looked at me as she said, "That is *so* sad." She paused briefly then inquired, "So you don't have any children?"

"Not human ones—just a very lovable canine child," I joked, secretly hoping this would end our conversation.

No such luck. She was relentless. "It's so very sad that you're all alone with no children to carry on your name." And then, as her eyes narrowed, she asked, "No girlfriend . . . or *anything?*"

"Well, I do have a significant other."

"Oh, that's good! What does she do?"

This woman will not give up. I took a deep breath as I tried to collect my thoughts (and stall a little) so as not to blurt out something I might regret. I always try to keep a low profile while on the job and use discretion in keeping my private life somewhat, well, you know, . . . private. However, when asked a direct question, I also won't lie. "Uh, *he* is an optician."

With that, she started shaking her head, repeating, "Tsk, tsk," over and over again. And then, "Sad . . . so very sad."

I tried to explain that I was involved in a long-term, loving, and committed relationship, but it fell on deaf ears. I guess she and her husband weren't so nice after all.

"Please come to our church sometime," the husband urged. "I think we can help you. We have a very successful conversion class."

I thanked them but said I already had a church.

"What *kind* of church?" She seemed incredulous.

"A wonderfully open and accepting church," I said.

"Tsk, tsk."

As I turned to keep making my way down the aisle, the husband pulled out a card and handed it to me. "Call me anytime," he said. "God would love for me to help you."

As I walked away, stuffing the card in my pocket until I could relocate it to its future home in the trash can, I couldn't help but think of *their* idea of happiness. They would probably consider the "me-me-me" woman and her husband a few rows ahead of them to be perfectly normal because they were "happily" married as husband and wife.

When I got to the galley, I pulled out the card to shred and dispose of it. But the picture on it caught my eye. The guy who was about to save me from eternal damnation was the assistant minister at a large, cultish gospel church in town. I ripped up the card and threw it in the garbage.

Done, I thought. *I'm not going to spend any more time even thinking about them.*

And I didn't—at least not until we landed in Chicago, cleared customs, and I boarded my bus for the three-hour ride home. I made my way toward the back of the bus, found a seat, sat down, and pulled out my inflatable neck pillow. As I started blowing it up, I heard, "Well, look who's back here! Isn't this something?" I looked up and saw His and Her Holiness. I half smiled as I kept blowing.

Although the bus was almost empty, they chose to sit right across the aisle from me. I had originally planned on reading for a while but then decided to take a nap first. I drifted off quickly and slept for an hour. When I opened my eyes, the wife was nodding off, but the husband was staring at me. I mean, *staring* at me.

This made me rather uncomfortable, so I faked a yawn and closed my eyes again. But by then, I was wide awake, so I decided to read. All the while, the husband just kept staring at me.

At one point, I glanced over, and he smiled at me, winked, and whispered, "Seriously, please call me sometime."

We couldn't have gotten to South Bend fast enough.

Over the next few months, I gave them very little thought, except when I passed their church on occasion. I wasn't sure why I even wasted any thought on them, but something kept nagging at me. That stare and wink while the wife was sleeping was just plain weird.

A little over a year later, while I was reading the newspaper, I turned the page and saw a photo of someone who looked oddly familiar. Of course, because it was a mug shot, it didn't capture the true essence of the person, who I suddenly realized was the good preacher man who'd wanted to convert me. Said preacher man had been arrested for soliciting an undercover cop at a local park—a *male* undercover cop.

I was surprised at how detailed the article was. The incident had taken place in the restroom at neighboring urinals. Allegedly, the defendant had solicited the undercover cop, who obviously either enjoyed this type of work or had simply drawn the short straw at the station earlier that day. While being questioned, the defendant had claimed he had bladder issues, so he had to "shake it" really hard. Upon further investigation, the article stated, this was his second arrest for the same offense. The first took place three years prior in a different state.

Shake it really hard? Oh, please! A child could've come up with a better excuse than that!

A few months later, as I was loading my purchases onto the conveyor belt at a local store, the cashier greeted me. Our eyes locked for several seconds, but his smile quickly faded as he recognized me. It was none other than Reverend Hypocrite.

There was a part of me that wanted to speak out and judge him right there, just like he and his wife had judged me. But I chose to take the high road and simply said, "Thank you" as he handed me my receipt.

As I was driving home, I couldn't help myself and drove by his church. His name was no longer on the sign. I figured the congregation must've forgotten what the Bible says about forgiveness. I wondered if his wife had too.

Tsk, tsk, I thought. *Sad . . . so very sad.*

Pea Ewe

By the late 1990s, I'd been a flight attendant for nearly two decades and had been working international flights for a few years. There were times when I had no words to describe how I felt. *Tired* just wasn't enough. *Exhausted* didn't quite cut it either without tacking on adverbs like *incredibly, absolutely, positively, completely,* or *totally. Tuckered out, pooped, drained*—all too cliché.

In one particularly grueling sixteen-day span, I completed five roundtrip international flights, zigzagging the globe as I traveled to Tokyo, Frankfurt, Rome, London, and Brussels. I felt like a human ping-pong ball as I bounced from one time zone to another.

By the time I departed for Brussels, it was starting to catch up with me. Due to weather, our departure from Chicago was five hours late, so we arrived in Brussels at two in the afternoon local time, which my body translated to seven o'clock in the morning. Once I was finally in my hotel room, I noticed how inviting the bed looked. That's the last thing I remember before waking up three hours later, splayed on top of the feather comforter, still fully dressed in my blue polyester uniform. I rolled over, squinted at the clock, and groaned, knowing I should get up. Otherwise, I knew I'd be in for a sleepless night.

As a flight attendant, getting enough sleep is always one of my greatest challenges, and I know I'm not alone. It's right up there with constipation. Over the years, I've learned to never *ever*—no matter how tired I am—nap for more than a couple hours after an all-night flight. I've only broken this self-imposed rule a few times, and on those memorable occasions, what little shut-eye I got during that nap proved to be the extent of my sleep over the course of almost three days. On those nights after a nap, I'd go back to bed, bleary-eyed and barely lucid, only to toss and turn for the next several hours. Finally, frustrated and cursing myself for having slept too much during the day, I'd get up and wonder how to pass the remainder of the night. There were usually two options: I could either read or watch some great middle-of-the-night foreign television. A person has not truly lived until watching *The Exorcist* in German, French, Spanish, and Italian. I thought it was a comedy the time I saw it in Japanese.

So, after this midafternoon nap in Brussels, I didn't want a repeat performance of those other sleepless nights. But when I looked out the window, a drizzly, gloomy day peered back. "A perfect day for sleeping," a small voice inside my head whispered. "Get up NOW!" another one shouted.

Finally, I stood up, unsteady on my feet. As I staggered to the bathroom, I paused in front of a mirror, horrified, yet slightly bemused, at what I saw. *How long have I been wearing this uniform? One day? Two?* I lifted my arm and took a whiff. *Whew! Peeling off this navy-blue costume will not be an easy task. No easier than peeling the skin from an underripe banana . . . Hmm . . . a banana,* I thought as a low grumbling sound emanated from the region of my belt buckle. It soon dawned on me how long it had been since I'd had anything to eat.

Food, although often the last thing on a jet-lagged person's mind, seems to balance out those pesky little circadian rhythms, allowing the proper neurons to fire at the right time. I snatched the room service menu from the desk and studied all the different entrées listed in French, Flemish, and English. My mouth fell open as I noticed the choices—and the prices.

**Salad of dried wild boar with a vinaigrette
of pig-sniffed truffles: $33**

Was the same poor pig used to sniff out the truffles from the ground before becoming the main ingredient in this side dish masquerading as an expensive entrée?

**Bruschetta of cinnamon-crusted red mullet
accompanied by an endive salad with a
hint of lavender and geranium: $42**

Is mullet a fish or a bad haircut? Can I justify spending forty-two dollars for a handful of greens and flowers—something I have in my own garden? Wouldn't it be cheaper just to graze when I get home?

**Boiled liver of a very young cow and curried potatoes
served with a brioche of capers and eggplant: $37**

A delicacy, I'm sure, but I think I'll wait until my next lifetime to find out.

Eel on a bed of creamed spinach with
two boiled potatoes: $27

Surely, I'll have sexual nightmares over this one.

Shank of mutton with peas and barley: $18

Could I get beyond the visual of some sheep hobbling around on three legs, while I pick the remnants of her fourth one out of my teeth?

Club sandwich and french fries: $19

Nineteen dollars! I can buy five club sandwiches at Denny's for that price—with fries and a bowl of soup!

In the end, my frugality won out. Call me a cheapskate or call me a sheep eater, but I needed something in my stomach, and I needed it without taking out a second mortgage on my house.

When the young man brought my tray, he smiled and said, "I hope ze meal is to your satisfaction, *monsieur.*"

"Thanks," I replied. "It sure smells good."

"Ah, yes, *monsieur.* Tell me, are you American?"

"I am."

"*Pardonnez-moi* for saying so, but ze Americans almost always order ze club sondwish. I am happy to see someone trying some-sing differ-ahhnt. Ze mutton and peas will create a symphony vis ze taste buds."

Just what I need—a bunch of racket in my mouth.

I tipped the gentleman and sat down to eat. From all appearances, the meal looked exquisite: beautifully garnished with larger-than-usual portions.

That must've been one big-assed sheep, I thought to myself. *Probably a mother*. I tried to picture something other than a gimpy sheep that would never be able to run freely with her lambs. It was all I could do to finish every last morsel. But I did. It was actually the first time I'd ever eaten mutton, lamb, or whatever it was.

Hoping to stay awake for a few more hours, I turned on the television. I channel surfed old American reruns, silently praying that I wouldn't suddenly come face-to-screen with Shari Lewis and Lamb Chop. I finally settled for *La Partridge Famille*. I watched, amazed, as Danny and Keith, in flawless French, argued with Reuben Kincaid over who deserved top billing.

"*Moi, Reuben, s'il vous plaît*," Keith pleaded.

"*Mais je suis le plus populaire*," argued Danny.

Then Laurie entered the room on the arm of her groovy new boyfriend. She ignored her brothers' bickering as the new guy whispered in her ear, "*Vous êtes jolie!*"

Although lacking originality, his compliment seemed to do the trick because within minutes, the two were lip-locked in what we were expected to believe was Laurie's first kiss—French-style. I wasn't fooled, however. Those tongues had met before.

Suddenly, Shirley, the mother of all mothers, burst into the room. Her exciting news quickly drowned out the arguing and slurping sounds. "*J'ai une surprise pour vous!*"

"*Qu'est-ce que c'est, Maman?*"

After hearing that they'd been asked to play a concert the following night at a juvenile detention center, the kids exclaimed in unison, "*C'est magnifique!*"

In the final minutes of the show, the members of the Partridge Family sang their hearts out to an unsmiling crowd of juvenile delinquents. And just as the room service guy had prom-ised, my own symphony began. Only it wasn't in my mouth.

At first, the sound was almost inaudible. It started as a low rumble in the depths of my mutton-and-pea-filled stomach. As I lay on the bed, I could actually see my extended belly start to move. *Was the sheep kicking me from inside my stomach?*

Within minutes, I sounded like a marching band. First, the drums commenced their cadence, then the horn section took over. I tooted like I'd never tooted before. I hit high notes, low notes, long, drawn-out, whole notes, and short, little pops. I cre-scendoed at well-timed intervals, absolutely amazed by my own musical ability.

I wonder if anyone in nearby rooms can hear me. Or nearby hotels, for that matter.

At times, my own gas actually rocketed me above the down comforter. On other occasions, after I got out of bed, I pro-pelled myself around the room. I quickly accepted the fact that the old adage, "Your own farts don't stink" was obviously cre-ated by someone lacking an olfactory sense. There may have been some rotten fish in Denmark, but on that night, there was something *really* rotten in Belgium. And it had taken up residence in my stomach.

Surprisingly, there was no discomfort or urgency to run to the toilet every few seconds. I did, however, run to the open window frequently to take in huge gulps of fresh air.

Despite my best efforts, my night proved to be a fitful one. I slept intermittently but kept waking myself up. I dreamed of three-legged sheep, bleating angrily at me. *Baaa! Baaa! Baaa-stard!*

Upon waking, I realized that the bleating wasn't just in my dream—it was coming from my rear orifice.

On international flights, lack of sleep isn't the only dilemma flight attendants face. Screaming passengers, seat duplications, backed-up lavatories, lengthy delays, and barfing children aside, one of the most common topics in galley conversations is regularity.

"Did you go today?"

"Any success on this layover?"

"Pellets or logs?"

"Do you have any Ex-lax in your tote bag?"

The sheer length of these flights tends to make us share our most intimate secrets, and I've had colleagues tell me they haven't "gone" in six days. This can be a major problem.

Back in Belgium, I sensed my own major problem brewing.

As I crossed the street to the airport on the morning after the mutton incident, I tooted freely but was drowned out by the roar of jet engines and honking taxicabs. As I passed through security, I squeezed my cheeks and hoped I wouldn't burst right there. Sweating profusely, I gingerly took baby steps through the checkpoint. Once on the other side, I expeditiously made my way to the nearest restroom, leaving my scent every step of the way.

How in the world will I ever make it to Chicago? I worried.

As we began to board the flight home, a young mother approached me to ask if we had a bathroom with a changing table.

"Yes, ma'am, right over there," I said, pointing to the closest lavatory.

She hoisted up her cargo, which happened to be one of the most perfect babies I had ever seen: perfect azure eyes as big and shiny as new quarters, perfect little dimples, a perfect toothless grin that would light up an entire 777, and perfect dark curls surrounding her perfect little face.

"She's perfect," I cooed.

"Oh, thank you. I just wish her stomach wasn't . . . well, so *sour* today. She's really gassy," the mother whispered apologetically.

"Oh, poor little thing." I tried to sound sincere as I felt the familiar rumble in my own gut.

She may have a sour tummy, I thought, *but she's still absolutely perfect in my eyes—a perfect baby and a perfect scapegoat.*

"Whoa! You'd better change her before takeoff. She needs a clean diaper pronto!" I loudly proclaimed. *Toot.*

"And we do have extra diapers on board. I have a feeling you're going to need a few." *Toot.* "Is she prone to stomach problems?" *Toot. Toot.*

Embarrassed, the poor mother quickly slipped into the nearest lavatory.

Over the next eight hours, I tried to save my crop-dusting for their section. Every time I strolled by, I marked my territory. Occasionally, I said loud enough for the neighboring ten rows to hear, "You might want to check her diaper. Poor little thing."

"But—" the young mother stammered.

"I know. *I* know," I interrupted, feigning compassion. "Sometimes their little tummies just can't take these long flights."

The young mother dashed off, red-faced, with her baby in tow. I smiled smugly as I roared down the aisle.

"Due to extremely strong tailwinds today," the captain soon announced, "we'll be arriving in Chicago twenty-five minutes early.

If he only knew.

Two days later, I was still backfiring. I was home by then, and even our precious pooch, Reggie, was keeping his distance. I was miserable as I realized I was approaching the Six Days Club. Trips to the bathroom became emotionally draining as I remembered the good times we once shared.

"Please, God. Just let me *go!*" I begged.

On the fourth day, my prayers were answered. I had just finished my cocktail of flaxseed, prune juice, and Absolut vodka when I felt my first contraction.

Could it be? I wondered.

Several minutes later, I felt a second. Then a third. Within half an hour, they were coming regularly. I hurriedly made a mental note of what I needed and then rushed around, retrieving the items.

A four-pack of Charmin. *Check.*

Glade Suddenly Spring air freshener. *Check.*

A plunger. *Check.*

A stack of reading material. *Check.*

Bucket, Scrubbing Bubbles toilet bowl cleaner, and brush. *Check, check, check.*

Just barely getting to the bathroom in time, I made myself as comfortable as possible. I began my deep-breathing exercises, grateful that I'd watched so many episodes of *ER*.

Breathe in . . . breathe out. In . . . out . . . in . . . out.

All of a sudden, I was overcome with pain. My breathing quickened. Within seconds, I was panting. I closed my eyes as I realized that the moment was near. I gritted my teeth and became my own coach. "Push," I grunted. "*PUSHHHH!*"

The pain, although excruciating for a split second, soon subsided and was replaced by a feeling of glorious release—incredibly, absolutely, positively, completely, and *totally* glorious.

I marveled at the size of my newborn. He—or was it a she?—must've weighed about eleven pounds and was at least eighteen inches long. *What a whopper!*

The dark complexion and green eyes bore no resemblance to me or Rich. *How will I explain this to family and friends? Should I send out announcements? Include a photo? There are so many things to consider, but for now, I just want to bask in the feeling of pure contentment.* Absentmindedly, I reached for the chrome handle and turned it.

The moment seemed surreal, frozen in time. *Flush!*

Although I heard it, I didn't immediately realize what I'd done. Then it slowly dawned on me. My eyes searched the bowl, but it was empty. *I* felt empty.

My grief was short-lived, though. A mere twenty-four hours following delivery, I was back in Brussels. Same hotel, same room service menu but eleven pounds lighter.

"Yes, *monsieur*, what may we bring you from ze room service menu?" asked a voice on the telephone.

Without hesitation, I replied, "I'll have the club sandwich."

Sometimes it's just worth the extra dollar to avoid all the crap.

A Cure for Crusty

I've never considered myself a prude. Far from it. I enjoy a good raunchy joke more often than not and have even been known to drop the F-bomb on occasion when no other word would suffice. I try never to use the Lord's name in vain, although I don't think he or she really minds. It's just something that was drilled into my head as a child at Vacation Bible School and stuck.

High school wasn't exactly a treasured experience for me. Coming from a small farming community, several of my fellow students went on to become farmers, truck drivers, factory workers, or ministers. It's not that I have anything against farmers, truck drivers, factory workers, or ministers. How could I since I added two of those to my résumé one summer during college? Since my hometown was just a few miles from the RV Capital of the World, it seemed befitting for me to work on the assembly line of a small factory, making window awnings for travel trailers. By summer's end, I had been promoted to deliveryman, partly because I was a good driver, but mainly because I was the only one besides the owner who'd never had a DUI. But try as I may, during my three months there, I never quite fit in.

"Hey, if one of you bastards is goin' to the break truck, get me a fuckin' cup of joe," never sounded quite right coming from me. I was more likely to say, "If you happen to be in the vicinity of the break truck, would you mind getting me a cup of coffee? And easy on the half-and-half, please and thank you."

And "Did you see the carnivorous bazongas on that new bitch in trim?" seemed a tad vulgar. "Did you happen to see how nicely that blouse complements the new gal in the trim department?" had a bit more finesse.

When I returned to college that fall, I soon realized that it wasn't a whole lot different than the factory.

"Hey, I porked a Sigma Cow last night. *Moooo!*"

I knew that in order to survive, I either had to acclimate and do the same or simply accept. I chose to accept.

Nothing though—no one, no way, no how—prepared me for a person I would later meet. Her name was Crusty McCrack-lin (obviously not her real name), and even the factory workers would've blushed around her.

By the time I met Crusty in 1996, I'd been working as a flight attendant for almost eighteen years. The airline had just started several new international routes out of Chicago, and one evening, as I was signing in for my trip to Zurich, I heard a commotion behind me. At least I thought it was a commotion. It was actually Crusty greeting another flight attendant she hadn't seen for some time.

"Oh my God, is that you, Shelley? I thought you'd fuckin' died or some shit. Damn, girl, you look good. Where the hell have you been?"

"Oh, hi Crusty. I just transferred here. I was in LA for twenty-five years."

"It's been twenty-five fuckin' years? Jesus H. Christ, I can't believe how time flies! It just frosts my tits."

"You're looking good, Crusty. You haven't changed a bit," Shelley replied.

After I turned discreetly to assess this Crusty person, I couldn't help but wonder how long it had been since Shelley had an eye exam. Crusty, quite literally, looked like a shar-pei in a flight attendant costume. Wrinkle upon tanned wrinkle adorned her face and chin, which were, thankfully, the only parts of her body showing. An unlit, no-filter Camel dangled from her crinkled, pencil-thin lips, no doubt waiting anxiously to be lit once she got to the nearby smoking room.

Her tone turned melancholy momentarily. "Aw shit, Shelley, that's real fuckin' sweet of you," she said around her cigarette. "Hey, you're not goin' to Zurich tonight, are you?"

"No, I'm on the Frankfurt trip."

"Dammit! Wouldn't that have been a fuckin' hoot if we could've flown together?"

It wasn't a fuckin' hoot to me, since I, not Shelley—lucky girl—was working the Zurich trip with Crusty. I was assigned as lowly coach scum on the flight, banished to the rear of the airplane, while Crusty—sweet, demure, classy Crusty—would be the purser and would work in first class. *It's going to be an interesting night.*

As I boarded the aircraft, I listened, rather than looked, for our fearless leader. But there wasn't a *shit, goddamn, bastard, hell,* or *motherfucker* to be heard. *Great,* I thought, *I can enjoy a moment's peace before all Crusty breaks loose.*

My thoughts quickly evaporated.

"*HEY!* You sons of bitches beat me to the goddamn plane! What kind of fuckin' purser am I, letting you pissants get on without my shit-for-brains guidance? Jesus, I'm showin' you bastards a hell of an example, aren't I?"

The sound of her deep-throated, nicotine-coated laughter permeated the cabin. It soon made way to a coughing fit. Once it had died down to an occasional guffaw, hack, and snort, I made my way to the source.

"Uh . . . , you must be Crusty. I'm Jim."

"Well, last time I looked in the goddamn mirror, I was Crusty. Nice to meet you, you cute little shit. Come to Mama." She whipped out her hand, hooked me by the back of the neck, then reeled me in to formally introduce my nose to her bosom.

Panic seized me as she held me tightly to her breast, and I feared I'd suffocate in her cleavage. But suddenly, I was released from my headlock as someone screamed, "Crusty, you old whore, how the *hell* have you been, girl?"

"OH MY GOD! You've got to be fuckin' shittin' me!"

I turned to look as Crusty and "Crustier" embraced one another.

"Cheryl, you old cunt, I thought you fell off the face of the motherfuckin' earth. Where the hell have you been?"

"Well, remember how they fuckin' fired me for that little incident on the flight from LaGuardia to Toronto a few years ago? I was on the beverage cart, mindin' my own fuckin' beeswax, when this little Jewish pip-squeak grabs my arm and says, 'Hey, stewardess, there's a fly in my kosher meal.' So I lean over his tray and scoop up the little fucker with a swizzle stick. Then I hold it up so I can get a *really* good look and I says, 'Well, he looks like he's circumcised, *and* he's wearing a yarmulke, so he must be kosher. What's the big deal?' That's it . . . That's all I said. And it took me two and a half years to get this fuckin' wonderful job back. Sometimes I wonder why I even bothered. So how have *you* been, girlfriend? You look awesome."

Awesome? I looked again, wondering if *I* was the one who needed my eyes checked.

After a few more minutes, we began to board the passengers, and for reasons unknown to any of us, Crusty perched herself near the entry door and slapped each of them on the back while making every inappropriate comment *verboten* from the flight attendant's bible.

"Where the hell do you plan on stickin' that cooler, dude?" she asked as she crossed her arms and stepped in the path of a skinny man with a long beard who was dressed in overalls and a flannel shirt.

The passenger eyed Crusty momentarily before she burst out laughing. "Don't *even* answer that unless you want these pointy-toed size 9 pumps up your scrawny ass!"

This was followed by more laughter and howling on both parts: the "professional" flight attendant and the dude who had apparently chosen to fly for the first time after missing his Greyhound bus.

But men weren't the only ones privy to Crusty's comments. "Ma'am, you'll find plenty of room for your hat in the overhead bin," she cooed.

"What? I'm not wearing a hat. This is my *hair*."

"Oh, of course it is. But you'll still find plenty of room in the overhead bin to store your hair, hat, or whatever the hell that is."

The lady with the poofy hair shuffled off, embarrassed. Her husband, however, found Crusty hysterical, and within seconds of her remark, the two were in each other's arms, laughing until they were crying. "How the hell do you sleep with *that?*" she screamed after him. The man went down the aisle, still wiping his eyes and snickering.

After some observation, I began to find Crusty somewhat entertaining. I even found ways to loiter around the boarding area so I wouldn't miss anything. That's when I saw a large man entering the aircraft.

"Good God, man! We'd better get you a couple seat belt extensions." When she looked at his boarding pass, she added, "Uh-uh . . . no way in *hell* are you sittin' in a window seat. We're gonna have to put you in an aisle seat; otherwise, the plane'll be bankin' to the right all the way to Zurich. We'll end up in Antarctica or some other shithole. Or worse yet, we'll just fly in circles all night."

Again, there were a few beats of silence followed by laughter and snorting as she threw a couple seat belt extensions at the passenger and ordered, "Go put these sons of bitches on! And no, you're *not* gettin' two meals tonight."

For the most part, the passengers loved her. *Most* of them, that is. When her first-class passengers began making their entrance, she purred, "Excuse me, sir. Do you and your daughter know where you're seated?"

"My *what?*"

"Oh, come on, Mac. Been there, done that. Woo-hoo! I'm just askin' if you know where your seat is."

"Well, I—"

"It's right back here, sir. And don't you worry. . . . I'm gonna take good care of you and the mistress—I mean missus . . . or whatever she is. You can bet on that."

Oh, she could be good.

While a princess was making her way down the jet bridge (not an actual member of a royal family, just a royal pain in the ass princess), Crusty looked her up one side and down the other and exclaimed, "Well, aren't *you* just a sight for sore eyes."

"Excuse me? And who, may I ask, are you?" Princess PITA eyed her disapprovingly.

"I, ma-*dam*, am your purser, Crusty."

"Crusty? Is that short for something?"

"Yes, 'tis, madam. Lady Elizabeth von Durenberg Crustingham. But you can just call me Crusty like all the other peons do."

"Well, Crrrr-usty, I'll need assistance placing my Louis Vwee-tohh bag in the . . . whatever you call it . . . overhead locker."

"Bin, m'lady. Bin."

"Whatever."

"Oh, thank you. And bless you, your highness. I'd be honored to take care of your Louis Vwee-tohh."

And as the honored guest found her way to 3H, Crusty stuffed the bag into the already full overhead bin.

About halfway into the flight, layover panic mode usually sets in—even for the Crusties.

What am I going to do on my layover?

Is the crew going to ditch me?

Will there be enough alcohol in Zurich to quench my thirst?

Are the tables in the hotel bar reinforced to hold my weight as I dance atop them and gyrate amongst the salt and pepper shakers?

Will I be able to sleep on my layover?

Will I be sleeping alone on my layover?

Will the forty cigarettes each crew member is allowed to bring into the country be sufficient?

Or will I need to make a withdrawal from my hidden cavity reserves?

Oh, so many dilemmas.

Just as I was contemplating my plans, I heard, "Hey, you little fucker! What are you doin' while you're in Zurich?"

I looked around and realized I was the only little fucker in the vicinity. "Me? Oh, I'm planning to go to Lake Zurich. They have a nice beach there."

I also knew it was a very European beach, meaning that clothing was optional. Although there were specific sections— bathing suits only, topless, bottomless, topless *and* bottomless, gay topless, gay bottomless, gay topless *and* bottomless—no rules were enforced. In other words, you could actually be a heterosexual woman who preferred to wear a top and no bottoms, sitting in the swimsuit-only gay section, and it was no big deal. No one blinked an eye.

On the other hand, I, being an American, blinked a lot behind my mirrored sunglasses. I liked to sit on the border between the gay and straight sections, with my head pivoting back and forth so as not to miss anything.

"The beach? Fuckin' A! Great idea! Maybe me and Cheryl can go with you. What time are you goin'?"

How do I get out of this? How do I get out of this?! I felt like a trapped animal. "I'm going . . . uh . . . right when we get in." I hated even saying it.

"Aw shit, man. I need some fuckin' shut-eye. These aren't natural good looks, ya know. I need some bee-yoooty sleep to look this fuckin' good. Hey, how 'bout we just catch up with you a little later?"

That could work, I thought. Apparently, she assumed it was a small beach area, and I decided to let her continue thinking that. I figured there was no way they could find me, especially behind my mirrored Foster Grants.

They found me.

Lying there, totally lost in the disco tunes emitting from my Sony Walkman, I almost threw out my back as a toe suddenly found a new home in my crotch.

"Hey, sailor, want some action?"

I squinted in the early afternoon sunlight, trying to focus on who was standing above me. Crusty and Cheryl plopped down, one on each side of me, and started to rip off their clothes, pour wine from their flasks, and light cigarettes—all at the same time.

"Well, you sneaky bastard. You were holdin' out on us. You didn't tell us this was a nudie beach. Far fuckin' out! I haven't been to a beach like this since these bastards were perky," she proclaimed, pointing to the breasts in her lap.

I followed her finger, and sure enough, she wasn't lying. Those bastards *were* no longer perky. They did, however, seem somewhat content as they rested comfortably on her thighs.

"These babies haven't seen the light of day in a long time."

I quickly scanned the area, hoping there was an escape route. "Unhook me, you little shit."

I took a deep breath, closed my eyes, and reached for her overburdened bathing suit top.

Slap! Slap! Although my eyes were still tightly closed, without even an inkling of curiosity or desire to peek, I instinctively knew the source of the sound: skin on skin.

I slowly opened my eyes to see a sight I wish I could forget: Crusty was sitting lotus-style with a cigarette dangling from her lips, a glass of wine in her hand, and wearing only her swimsuit bottoms. I suddenly remembered why I was gay.

"Goddamn, that feels good!" she proclaimed. "Come on, Cheryl, you prissy-assed prude. I'm not gonna be the only one sittin' here topless while all those sons of bitches are oglin' me."

Ogling? I thought. I looked around and realized we'd soon have a lot more room to spread out because several groups were making hasty exits.

Not to be outdone by a sexpot like Crusty, Cheryl had her top off before Crusty could light another cigarette.

Several times in my life I've found myself in a situation, wondering, *How did I get myself into this? And how do I get out of it?* This was one of those times.

"Hey, Jim, why don't you take that Speedo off and give Mama an eyeful?"

I smiled as I pointed to my headphones. Shrugging, I mouthed, "I can't hear you."

"I SAID, 'WHY DON'T YOU TAKE OFF THAT FUCKIN' BATHING SUIT! IT'S NOT LIKE YOU'RE HIDIN' ANYTHING. I CAN PRACTICALLY SEE YOUR TALLYWACKER THROUGH IT!'"

I looked around, wishing I were invisible. More people were leaving. *At this rate, the whole beach will be clear within an hour.*

"Aw fuck, man, this feels so . . . so invigoratin'," Crusty remarked as she put another cigarette in her mouth, freeing her hands and reaching for her breasts. As she juggled them like two overripe watermelons, she suddenly became reflective. "Not bad for fifty-two, huh?"

Is she talking about her age or her boob size? I wondered. *Is there such a thing as 52 long?*

Next, it was Cheryl's turn. "Well, these puppies aren't so bad either, are they, Jim? Even though you're . . . well, you know. You can still appreciate feminine beauty, right?"

I can when I see it. But it wasn't anywhere in my line of vision.

"Well, most men would come crawlin' for these babies," Cheryl purred.

Crawling would probably be the best approach since, like Crusty, Cheryl had some low-hanging fruit.

"But you know what? That fuckin' son of a bitch slime bag I married doesn't want me anymore. Says I don't have what he *needs*. That's bullshit, isn't it, Crusty?"

Cheryl didn't wait for an answer before the waterworks began. "I need more wine," she sniffled as she reached for her flask. She then started sobbing uncontrollably. Her shoulders shook and shuddered as she gulped air, all the while keeping a cigarette safely pressed between her quivering lips.

"Aw shit, Cheryl, don't start blubberin'," Crusty said, reaching for her own flask. "Keep that up, and I'll be bawlin' right along with you. You know what a sweet, sensitive bitch I am."

For the next three hours, I became a slightly inebriated, Speedo-clad version of Dr. Phil. I heard all about the lives of Crusty and Cheryl—from start to the present. It's true that alcohol erases inhibitions because I heard *way* more than I wanted.

At times, Cheryl and Crusty seemed to be the best of friends, but at other times, they'd lash out at each other. One-upping seemed like a game to them.

"Well, maybe your old man is a motherfucker, but I bet *you've* never found him in bed with your sister!" Cheryl cried.

"Just *one* of my sisters?" Crusty questioned. She squinted as she took a long drag from her Camel and blew it out the corner of her mouth.

"I only *have* one sister," Cheryl retorted.

"Too bad. I've caught my dickhead in the sack with both of mine."

"Well, *shit*. He gave me the crabs one time."

"Try crabs and fuckin' gonorrhea at the same motherfuckin' time. I almost clawed my twat out!"

"Well, *my* dickhead almost clawed my goddamn heart out." Still sobbing, Cheryl wiped the spittle from the corner of her mouth.

"Oh, come here, hon," Crusty said reassuringly as she pulled Cheryl in for a bare-chested embrace. It was quite touching. Literally.

I looked away, somewhat embarrassed, feeling like I was witnessing something very private. The feeling was short-lived, however, because a new scene suddenly presented itself. A naked, older man was slowly making his way back from the toilet. As he walked past us and approached his blanket, which happened to be about five feet from us, he spotted his can of lager still sitting next to his tattered underwear. He eyed it for a moment, no doubt trying to focus on it, before bending over to pick it up. As he reached out to grab the can, he stumbled, catching himself just before going down. I was mesmerized. Crusty and Cheryl must've been too because they pulled away from each other. We were all witnessing something normally saved only for the eyes of a well-seasoned proctologist.

We watched those suckers sway, back and forth, back and forth. I was becoming seasick, so I hurriedly looked for a large, stationary item to focus on. I settled on Crusty's right nipple, which was the size of a bread plate.

"Hey, big guy, you need some help?"

I looked around, wondering where this expletive-free question had come from. *Certainly,* I thought, *it could not have been Crusty or Cheryl.*

"You shpeak Ainglish, Schatz?" the man asked, trying to focus on Crusty as he grabbed his ball sack midswing.

"No shit, Sherlock." Crusty smiled and looked down, trying to appear demure.

"I haf anozzah beer if you vould like it."

"Ooh, I bet you have something else I would like, *mein Herr,*" Crusty sounded almost sexy—in a middle-aged, beer-guzzling, smokes three packs a day sort of way.

He smiled back at her, revealing that he was long overdue for a dental checkup. "Und I sink you haf somezing I vould like too . . . *mein schönes Fräulein.*"

That's all it took. Crusty quickly got to her feet, Herr staggered in her direction, and they were off.

"Your place or mine?" Crusty blinked her bloodshot bedroom eyes at him.

"Hey, bitch, you're not leavin' our sorry asses here alone!" Cheryl bellowed as she gulped down the last of her wine, then jumped to her feet. "I'm gettin' a piece of this too!"

Shortly, we were all packed up, dressed (thankfully), and on our way to the bus stop.

Herr looked at his scrumptious prizes and grinned. "Ah ladies, I haf somezing in shtore for you tonight. You vill love it."

"Do I need to go back and freshen up? You know, put on a new fuckin' face?"

And a new body, perhaps, I thought.

"Oh no, Schatz. Your face is *perfekt*."

As we approached the bus stop, Crusty had one arm looped through Herr's; in the other, she carried a beer. It was a romantic sight. In fact, I got teary-eyed for a moment, but then I looked at my watch. "Oh my gosh! Is it five o'clock? I've got to get back to the hotel." No one even blinked a bloodshot eye. "I'm meeting a friend for dinner," I lied. They couldn't have cared less. They had more urgent issues.

"*Mein Herr*," Crusty said, looking at her new prince, "what the hell *is* your name anyway?"

"Rudolph, but you can call me Rudy."

"Like the fuckin' red-nosed reindeer?" Crusty doubled over. "What a fuckin' hoot! Hey, if you're named after a reindeer, are you hung like one? Oh, wait! I've already seen that son of a bitch, and it's hangin' down to your knees!"

Crusty and Cheryl fell into each other's arms, laughing.

"You von't be disappointed," replied the sleazeball.

"Well! Gotta go!" I couldn't get out of there fast enough. "See you tomorrow morning." I don't think they even noticed me leave.

There was a part of me that felt just a tad bit guilty for abandoning these two helpless ladies in the company of the Swiss Casanova. But there was another part of me that thought, *Run as fast as you can. And don't look back!*

The rest of the night was peaceful. No boobs, no dangling balls, no fuckin' this and fuckin' that—just a nice quiet evening alone in my hotel room. I went to bed early since I hadn't gotten my customary nap at the beach, thanks to Crusty and Cheryl.

I was in a deep sleep when a banging on the door suddenly ripped me from my slumber. I grabbed my pants and rushed to the peephole, wondering who was on the other side. Before I could focus, I knew.

"Let me in, you little horse's ass!"

I opened the door a crack, ensuring that the security chain was locked and in place. "Crusty, is something wrong?"

"You're sure as hell right something is wrong!" she cackled. "I need a drink!"

"But Crusty, it's two o'clock in the morning." I reluctantly closed the door and took the chain off.

"Who the hell cares? Are you gonna turn into a fuckin' pumpkin?" she asked as I opened the door.

"Uh . . . no. But I'd kinda like to get some sleep before our eight o'clock pickup," I yawned.

"Hell, you can always sleep at home."

With that, she pushed past me and headed for my minibar. She pulled out a couple of scotches and poured herself a hefty glass before plopping down on the bed.

"Well, that Rudy was one fuckin' nutball. Couldn't even get it up after all those promises." After taking a sip of scotch, she pulled out a cigarette. Then she squinted as she looked around the room. "Where the hell's an ashtray?"

"This is a nonsmoking room," I stated.

"Well, go grab me a glass, and put a little water in the son of a bitch!" she ordered. "They think they're so goddamn smart."

No problem, I thought, *I'll just use a credit card when I check out. I probably won't have enough cash anyway, since my bill will now include two scotches at ten dollars a pop and a fine of two hundred Swiss francs for smoking in a nonsmoking room.*

I looked from the cloud of smoke that encased Crusty to my alarm clock on the nightstand. It was 2:12 a.m. Realizing that I was more than likely done sleeping for the night, I got up and grabbed a beer from the minibar. *What's another eight dollars at this point?*

For the next two hours, Crusty regaled me with every last detail of her evening, ending with, "And after all that, I didn't even get laid, God dammit! I'm *really* hot and bothered now!"

Her eyes focused on me as she gave me a lopsided grin, which ensured that her dangling cigarette wouldn't fall from its happy home on the other side of her mouth. When she finally got to her feet after two failed attempts, she staggered toward me, knocking over a chair and tripping over the wastebasket along the way. As the gap between us grew smaller, I began to get nervous.

"Get over here, baby boy! Mama needs some lovin'!"

"Uh, Crusty, I don't think—"

"Come over here," she purred. "I know you're gay and all that shit, but tonight, you're gonna fuck me. And you're gonna *love* it!"

After I politely refused, Crusty became somewhat belligerent, perhaps because I was the second man who couldn't—or wouldn't—get it up for her that day. So I walked to the door, opened it, and stepped into the hallway, hoping she'd follow. She did, but she called me every name in the book, which, in her book, was *a lot* of names.

Her reflexes were quite a bit slower than mine, so she didn't make it back into the room before I slammed the door. In retrospect, that might not have been the right thing to do because I realized quickly that a drunk and horny Crusty is much louder and more aggressive than a sober Crusty. She banged on the door and screamed for several minutes, but then suddenly, she quieted down, and I heard men's voices. After that, total silence. I waited a minute before peeking out the door to see two of the hotel's security guards leading her to the elevators.

Needless to say, I never slept another wink that night. I lay there wondering what the repercussions would be the next day.

At 7:59 a.m., I reluctantly left my room and went to the lobby, prepared for the worst. When I got off the elevator, the whole crew was standing by the exit doors, with Crusty holding court in the middle of the group. When she spotted me, she yelled, "Good mornin', you little shit! Come give me a hug!" She seemed chipper and looked surprisingly rested for the couple hours of sleep she might've gotten. I wondered if she had any recollection of what had happened in my room, but I certainly wasn't going to ask or remind her.

The trip back to Chicago was uneventful. It wasn't quiet by any means—that wasn't possible with Crusty on board. I watched her, amazed that she could function so well after drinking so much and getting so little sleep.

When we arrived back in Chicago, I was one of the last people off the airplane. As I was exiting customs, Crusty stood on the other side, waiting for me.

"I didn't want to run off without sayin' goodbye," she said. "Come fly with Mama anytime, you little shit! I love the fuck outta you!" I think that translated to, "I really enjoyed working with you. Let's do it again." We hugged and went our separate ways.

Over the years, I flew with Crusty several more times. None was quite as bizarre as the first time, but none was ever boring either. That was just Crusty. Several years later, when I heard she'd retired, it was bittersweet because there was something very likable about her. But it was also a relief of sorts knowing that I'd never again have to wince when I heard what came out of her mouth.

Then, out of the clear blue, I got a phone call from her one day. She had just talked to a good friend of mine and had gotten my number. For the first part of the conversation, we reminisced and laughed about the memories we shared. I was a little nervous she might bring up "that" night, but she never did. She told me she had retired because her longtime boyfriend had passed away unexpectedly. That really came as a surprise to me because I never knew she had a longtime boyfriend. She had mentioned her "old man, the motherfucker" a few times, but I just assumed they were just casual friends with benefits. They'd obviously been a couple for many years, though, because they owned two homes together. When he died suddenly, she said she'd felt overwhelmed by everything, so she decided to retire. She said she'd spent the first several months after his death readying one of the houses to sell. Right after the sale was finalized, she found out she had stage 4 breast cancer. She had a double mastectomy and several months of aggressive treatment, which had ended a year prior.

I asked her if she still heard from Cheryl, and she laughed. "Hell yeah, I do. I not only hear from her, I just saw that bitch a couple months ago. She flew in to see me. She finally divorced that asshole she was married to."

When I asked if they still partied a lot, she replied, "Nah, not really. When I found out I had cancer, I quit smokin' cold fuckin' turkey. Those sons of bitches were killin' me. And I only have a glass of wine once in a blue moon. I guess I've turned into one of those borin'-ass bastards I used to make fun of."

She was still Crusty, but there was something noticeably different about her. She still used her expletives, no doubt about that, but there seemed to be fewer *motherfuckers* and *goddamns*. And when she did use them, her tone seemed much softer.

She said that after her boyfriend died, one of the insurance companies tried to get out of paying his life insurance policy. Even though she was his beneficiary and common-law spouse, they stalled in settling. "I fought those motherfuckers big-time. They didn't know who the hell they were dealin' with."

But then she suddenly grew reflective, "I decided right then and there that because of those dumb shits, I'm leavin' every goddamn cent I have to shelters and pet rescue charities."

I smiled as I remembered the first time I met her. In some ways she was the same; in others, she was so very different. But she was still dear Crusty, the crude, rude, fighting machine with a heart of pure gold.

A New
Attitude

The sounds of chainsaws and a backhoe were not exactly what I wanted to wake up to at six o'clock in the morning, especially since I hadn't gotten home from a long trip until eleven thirty the night before. As I slowly hauled myself out of bed to find the source of the racket, I was a bit taken aback when I opened the blinds and found myself face-to-face with a Porta-Potty. You know, one of those blue, portable, smelly numbers often seen at county fairs, family reunions, and NASCAR races. In the right place, they're functional and necessary. But seven feet from your bedroom window is never the right place.

The fact that it was so close to my bedroom window was a bit of a surprise, but the reason was not. When Rich and I moved into our new home the previous year, there was a large, wooded area between us and the main entrance to the subdivision. It was comprised of three separate lots, and the real estate agent, who also happened to own the land, told us it might sell "within the next several years." As it turned out, the lot closest to us sold within months, so I knew it was just a matter of time before construction started. Even so, I wasn't quite ready for the sounds associated with clearing the lot and building a house—not at the crack of dawn anyway.

Maybe I'm overreacting a bit. After all, I'll be traveling a lot in the next few months, and really, how long does it take to build a house? Six, seven months? Eight at the most?

I couldn't help but wonder, though, if waking up to a crapper outside my window might somehow be foreshadowing the day ahead of me. Just to be on the safe side, I decided to tweak my usual morning affirmation of, "Today will be perfect in every way" to "It's not going to be a crappy day. It's not going to be a crappy day. It's *not* going to be a crappy day."

By this time I was wide awake, so I decided to get up. Besides, I had a lot to do on my one and only day off that week. I made some coffee and sat down to write a list of everything that needed to be done. Having been gone for a week and a half, I had several errands to run. But first and foremost, I had promised to take my aunt to the airport. She'd been visiting from Tennessee for the past two weeks and was scheduled to leave later that morning. I had volunteered to take her so I could spend some more time with her before she left. I phoned my mother's house, where my aunt was staying.

"Hi, Auntie Mert," I said when she answered. *Why hadn't I been more creative when I'd given her that nickname forty-some years before?* "It's Jim." *Like someone else would be calling her Auntie Mert?* We chatted for a few minutes before I asked, "Would you like to have breakfast before your flight?"

"That would be peachy. I'm all packed and just sittin' here watchin' paint dry," she said in her acquired southern drawl."

"Okay, I'll be there in about an hour."

I quickly got ready and was on my way in twenty-five minutes. When I arrived and gave Auntie Mert a big hug, she said, "Uh . . . I wouldn't squeeze too hard if I were you."

"Why not?" I just *had* to ask.

"Well, . . . I just hope I can make it to the airport without . . . uh . . . you know . . ."

No, I didn't know. I had a good idea of what she might be talking about since this side of my family had a tendency to share, shall we say, very *intimate* details with one another about a certain subject. Details concerning frequency, consistency, and color.

"I crapped my pants last night! We'd just barely made it back from El Taco Grandy; otherwise, I would've messed in your mom's car. You know I love Mexican food, but it just tears me up."

"Grande," I corrected.

"Huh?" she asked, as she gingerly walked toward her suitcase.

"It's pronounced gr-r-r-ande," I said, perfectly trilling my *r*'s.

"Oh, okay . . . gr-r-r-andy!"

As I drove, I kept a close watch on Auntie Mert. We laughed and shared stories during the half-hour trip to the restaurant. I tried to keep the laughter to a minimum, though, since I hadn't had the chance to cover the passenger seat with a plastic tarp.

We enjoyed a nice, bland, and uneventful breakfast, then headed to the airport. I parked my car and insisted on carrying all of Auntie Mert's bags, not quite sure what lifting, pulling, or pushing might do to her. After checking in at the front ticket counter, we were directed to the security screeners. I flashed my airline ID and was nodded through by the Barney Fife on duty.

As I hoisted Auntie Mert's bags onto the conveyor belt, I had a flashback of a conversation we'd had at breakfast.

"Do you have extra underwear in your carry-on bag?" I'd discreetly asked.

"Good Lord, yes. I always do. You just never know when something like this will happen."

I had to admit she was right. Just then, a loud beeping at the security station brought me back to the present moment.

"Ma'am, could you step over here for a moment?" an absolutely expressionless and somewhat masculine-looking woman in a black uniform said to my aunt. "For some reason, you've set off the sensor, so you'll need to be wanded."

"And sir, you'll need to open all of your bags for inspection," Barney said to me in a booming voice. "Please just stand over here until we finish with her."

"Her" happened to be an elderly woman who resembled a bag lady. She had every designer bag in the world: Target, Kmart, Walmart, JCPenney. And each one was overflowing with absolute necessities she would no doubt need on the fifty-minute flight to Cincinnati.

As Auntie Mert was ushered behind a curtain for her cavity search, I eavesdropped on the Bag Lady's conversation with Barney.

"Is this the train to Cleveland?" she cackled.

"Uh, ma'am, your boarding pass says you're *flying* to *Cincinnati*," he responded, eyeing her suspiciously.

"That's what I said," she retorted. "Hey, you want a kumquat?"

"Uh, no, thank you. Do you have a cell phone in your bag?"

"Yep, it's in one of 'em."

"Can you show it to me?"

"Show you what?"

Oh great, maybe I should just drive Auntie Mert to Cincinnati. Even if I took her all the way to Nashville, we'd probably get there sooner.

"What is this, ma'am?"

"It's the remote for my TV."

"And this?"

"A mousetrap."

I quickly peeked over at the curtain, wondering what was happening to my poor aunt.

"Sir, is this your bag?" Barney asked.

Hallelujah! It was my turn.

Now, it wasn't *technically* my bag, but in the interest of expediting this security drama, I figured I should claim it as my own. Besides, I knew my aunt well enough to know that she always followed the rules verbatim and would never pack any sharp or questionable items.

"Yes, that's my bag," I fibbed, crossing my fingers.

"Would you please unzip it?"

After I did, Barney plunged his hand inside the bag long enough to retrieve a pair of white, size 14, Hanes Her Way cotton briefs.

"Are these yours?" he smirked.

I could feel my face reddening. "Well, kind of, . . . sir."

"What do you mean *kind* of?"

Before I could answer, his hand took another nosedive into the paisley print bag, where he found a new treasure: a box of extra-absorbent pantyliners.

"And these? . . . Yours too?"

"Well, uh . . ."

By this time, he was on a mission. Out came the prescription bottle containing "my" hormones. And the makeup pouch, curlers, and denture adhesive. With each newfound discovery, he sneered and looked at me questioningly.

Okay, so I'm a denture-wearing, hormonal cross-dresser with a leakage problem who likes curly hair! I wanted to scream. But instead, I showed him my airline badge again and tried to explain that I was just assisting my aunt to her gate.

That's when he ripped into me, scolding me for at least five minutes. "You're an airline employee? You should know better! You *cannot* carry someone else's personal items through security! What if she had a bomb or a gun in her bag?"

I apologized profusely, doubting Auntie Mert had either a bomb or a gun in her bag. The only thing in danger of exploding was in her drawers.

Shaking his head, he suddenly said, "Sorry, didn't mean to be so hard on you, but you know the rules. Just don't let it happen again."

I held my head in shame as he waved me through.

Just then, Auntie Mert emerged from behind the curtain and remarked, "Well, she sure was a nice gal."

"Was there another woman back there assisting?" I asked as I remembered Stone Face who had taken her back.

"Oh no, it was just me and Melissa. I told her all about my fake knee and even showed her my scar. Did you know she just had a hysterectomy three months ago? She said her periods had become really irregular."

Good God, I thought. *What* didn't *you two talk about?*

"I told her all about my diarrhea episode too. Didn't you hear us laughin'?"

I told her I hadn't because I was too busy trying to explain the goodies in "my" bag. Then I asked if she'd seen Bag Lady. She hadn't, so I pointed her out. Even without my help, she would've been pretty easy to spot. The airplane for the Cincinnati flight seated a total of sixteen passengers, uncomfortably, so the boarding area consisted of me, Auntie Mert, seven businessmen, and the Bag Lady. It seemed like a pretty simple deduction.

"I sure hope she's not sitting next to you," I whispered.

"Why not?" Auntie Mert asked innocently. "She looks sweet. Poor thing must've lost something," she said as we watched the woman rifle through her bags.

Why can't I be more like Auntie Mert? She always seems to find the good in people.

When the agent made the boarding announcement, the passengers began lining up at the gate. I stood to the side, next to Auntie Mert. As we began moving forward, our quiet conversation was suddenly interrupted.

"Are you goin' to Dayton?" someone asked over the sound of rustling plastic bags.

"Well, no, I'm goin' to Cincinnati then on to Nashville," laughed Auntie Mert. "Aren't you goin' to Cincinnati too?"

"Yeah, okay. But guess what! I forgot to put my bra on this morning. So I threw it in my Walmart bag. Or was it my Kmart bag? Either way, now I can't find it."

Auntie Mert smiled as she leaned in closer. "Well, I had diarrhea all night, so I just hope I don't have any accidents on the plane."

The two women howled. A friendship was blossoming.

As they strolled down the jet bridge lost in conversation, I smiled, waved one last time, and said a silent prayer that there was a bathroom on the small puddle jumper.

Driving out of the airport parking lot, I looked at my to-do list and thought, *How in the world am I going to get everything done before leaving town tomorrow?*

Breakfast
Airport
Work out
Get groceries
Chiropractor
Have tire fixed
Clean house
Do laundry
Pick up uniform

At least I can check off the first two items. Maybe I should just pri-oritize the others in order of importance, and the rest can wait. Okay, I really don't have to work out today—there's always next week. Plus, it's probably not a good idea to exercise just yet since I threw out my back a few days ago. It could actually make it worse. And it's not absolutely nec-essary to go to the chiropractor. Although it still hurts a bit, the spasms have subsided, so I can live with it a little while longer.

There's really no rush on the tire either. The screw lodged in my right front tire has been there for several days, so it's not a huge threat or any-thing. It hasn't even lost any air. I'll just have it fixed when I get back, maybe the same day I go to the gym and chiropractor, since they're all in the same vicinity.

And other than dinner tonight and breakfast tomorrow, we're not in dire need of food. I can just stop and get the bare necessities. If Rich gets hungry while I'm gone, he'll eventually figure out where the nearest supermarket is. And there's always fast food.

While I was contemplating what absolutely *had* to be done, common sense started whispering in my ear that it would be just plain stupid to even try to clean the house and do the laundry, what with my bad back and all.

By the time I'd revised my list, only one thing remained: Pick up uniform.

As I was passing the mall on my way to the dry cleaner, on a whim, I turned into the parking lot. Having updated my to-do list, I pretty much had the rest of the day free. Besides, I needed some new jeans because all my other ones had apparently shrunk or were in the dirty clothes hamper.

I found a parking spot in front of Macy's and headed inside. As I was making my way toward the men's department, a heavily made-up woman—who, according to her name tag, was "KimberLeigh"—stepped out from behind a cosmetics counter. "Good afternoon, sir. May I offer you a sample of our new moisturizer?"

"No, thank you," I said because I'd already applied my tried-and-true lotion that morning.

"You could certainly benefit from it," she smiled insincerely as she blocked my path.

"Uh, no. But thank you."

KimberLeigh could not be stopped. "Are you a farmer?" she asked, putting on her glasses and studying my face.

"A farmer? No, why do you ask?"

"Did you used to be a lifeguard?"

"A lifeguard? No. Why?"

"Well, you just have that weathered look . . . like you've spent *a lot* of time outdoors."

I was really starting to dislike KimberLeigh.

"I wholeheartedly believe this product could help reverse some of the damage," she continued. "And we have a great concealer for those dark circles under your eyes."

"Thanks, but—"

"Please have a seat here," she motioned to a stool in front of the counter.

Ten minutes and ninety-two dollars later, I left the store. I was no longer in the mood to shop for jeans. As I walked to my car, I examined my receipt, wondering how I'd spent almost a hundred bucks in such a short time. I was so engrossed in the receipt that I didn't see the curb until I tripped over it, landing hard on my ass with an audible *CRAAACK*. I quickly got up and scanned the parking lot, praying no one had seen me.

I drove to the dry cleaner, picked up my uniform, and then ran into the grocery store. As I was leaving the store with my groceries in hand, something seemed odd about my car. *Is it leaning to the right?* I asked myself. I walked around the front of the car, and sure enough, my front right tire was flatter than a pancake. *It must've needed more immediate attention than I thought.* I opened the trunk and tried to guess where the jack and lug wrench might be hiding. Once I found them, I retrieved the owner's manual from my glove box and flipped to "Quick and Easy Steps for Changing a Tire." An hour and a half later, I was finally on the road again with the spare tire in place, hoping my nuts were tight and that, by the grace of God, the tire shop was still open.

A few minutes later, I pulled in at the tire store and parked my lopsided car. I tried the front door of the shop, but it was locked. As I started walking dejectedly back to my car, someone opened the door and yelled, "Do you need something?"

I turned and saw a man standing there. When I told him about the tire, he said, "We just closed, but I can take a look at it."

I felt a tinge of guilt. The man's hands were covered in dirt, grease, tar, and whatever else is on old, worn tires, and he had the deep-lined, tired faced of someone who worked hard and rested little. KimberLeigh would've had a field day with him. He shuffled over to my car, looked at the tire, and told me to pull it into the bay. Within minutes, he had fixed the flat. I pulled out my wallet, but he shook his head and said, "No charge, my friend. You're my last customer of the day."

I thanked him and got into my car. As I pulled out onto the busy street, I wondered why this perfect stranger hadn't charged me. There was absolutely nothing in it for him. Or was there? Then I thought about Auntie Mert and her kindness to the two people I'd judged prematurely. They had both obviously benefited from her joyful spirit. And even KimberLeigh, despite her abruptness and brutal honesty, had helped guide me to a new regimen that would undoubtedly erase ten or twenty years from my old and weathered face.

Lost in my thoughts and with the sun in my eyes, I almost didn't see the stopped bus in front of me. Slamming on the brakes of my Corolla and skidding several yards, I stopped no more than an inch or two from the huge vehicle.

When I arrived home a few minutes later, I was still shaking but very thankful that I hadn't kissed the tail end of a bus. Had I not seen it exactly when I did, the situation could've had a very ugly ending. And as I lifted the groceries out of the trunk, I suddenly realized that my back pain was completely gone. Not even a twinge. *Perhaps my spill in the parking lot earlier actually knocked something back into place.*

While preparing dinner, the phone rang. It was a good friend and colleague that I'd be working with the following day. "Did you see that our Frankfurt trip for tomorrow was canceled?"

I hadn't. I immediately thought of the pay I'd be losing.

"It's the twenty-eighth of the month, and there are no other trips available, so be sure to put yourself on the makeup list."

That was music to my ears because if we had a trip canceled in the last five days of the month and we made ourselves available for another trip, we were paid for the trip. And because all the other flights were already covered, I'd have a paid, week-long mini-vacation. *I can get all the things from my original list done, plus some.*

What a wonderful day it had been. It hadn't been crappy at all.

Prisoners
to a Cell

In the early 2000s, an Internet petition was circulating, asking to ban cell phone usage on airplanes. I copied, pasted, and signed it faster than a teenage girl texting her bestie and forwarded it to everyone I knew on social media. I couldn't imagine what sort of monster the use of cell phones on planes might unleash in an already cramped and testy environment.

Delayed departures, barfing children, lightning strikes at thirty thousand feet, enough flatulence to cause oxygen masks to drop, inoperative video screens, and obese passengers spewing into neighboring seats would pale in comparison to the horrors that using cell phones on airplanes would generate. Air travel would reach a whole new level of insanity. Brawls would ensue between passengers angry with the noise level of phones ringing and people talking. Flight attendants would become referees. We'd be handing out earplugs instead of pretzels.

I don't even want to imagine that.

Now, don't get me wrong, I'd be absolutely lost without my iPhone. It's as much a necessity when commuting to Chicago by car as my travel urinal, Donna Summer CDs, and 3 Musketeers bars.

Because of the ever-increasing capabilities of this incredible technology, countless problems are no doubt solved every moment of every day. It makes me wonder how we ever lived without them.

But many have taken this one-time luxury to a whole new level. I've heard what should be private conversations in five-star restaurants, health clubs, department stores, fast-food joints, bathrooms, supermarkets, movie theaters, churches, funeral homes, gas stations, hospitals, and doctors' offices.

God forbid the woman wearing yoga pants that are stretched to the max and screaming for mercy and a 3X Elvis T-shirt proclaiming to the world that she's a "Hunka Burning Love" could possibly make her own decision on whether to get little Stacy size 22 or 24 underwear at Walmart without calling her a few times. Apparently, it doesn't even cross her mind that if she goes over her monthly minutes again, she could risk losing her 1973, twelve-by-sixty-foot trailer, the fancy model with the sagging pop-out dining room where Stacy likes to hang out.

No, she doesn't seem to be worried that her phone charges are racking up. After all, Stacy is pregnant again, so her food stamps will take care of all the healthy staples: doughnuts, cookies, candy, soda, and disposable diapers for the two she's already cranked out. Shouldn't be a problem at all, especially since Hunka Burning Love is working part-time at the gas station, ensuring that she has enough money for all the other necessities: beer, cigarettes, and lottery tickets. She's even been able to put a little aside for unforeseen expenses, like another flat tire on the house.

From what I've gathered inadvertently listening to their conversation, Mama and Stacy have prevented countless disasters thanks to their cell phones—disasters of mammoth proportions, just like the one I heard that day.

"So do you want HoHos or Little Debbies?" I heard Mama Hunka Burning Love scream into the phone. She paused, as her tongue seemingly searched her toothless gums for any leftover remains from her lunchtime Whopper.

"No, dammit, I ain't buyin' you no more Twinkies. I seen you ate the last of 'em, and I don't care if you *are* eatin' for two—I ain't buyin' you no more Twinkies! If your ass gets any bigger, we're gonna have to get a double-wide." After a momentary pause, she continued, "Don't yell at me, you little bitch! I AIN'T gettin' you no more Twinkies!"

And then calmly, "They're out of the Hi-C and Bugles we seen in the ad. They'll give me a rain check, but I ain't waitin' no week. You know that doctor said you have to drink more fresh juice and eat more roughage. So I guess I better run over to Kmart and see if they got any. I'll call ya from there."

She quietly listened for a handful of seconds before bellowing, "God DAMMIT, Stacy! I told you, I AIN'T gettin' you no Twinkies! You keep it up, and you're gonna eat me right out of house and home."

Trailer, I want to correct her. *Trailer* and home.

"Okay then, bye. Love you too, hon. I'll call ya from Kmart."

One time, I was sitting alone in a restaurant just before Christmas, enjoying a quiet lunch, when I suddenly heard a muffled version of "Jingle Bells." I quickly realized it was someone's phone ringing.

"Hello . . . hello? Hello. . . . Hellooo? Oh, hi! No, I just had lunch. . . . No, no, I just couldn't find my phone. It was buried in my purse under my headscarf. No, no. You don't have to call back later. You're not bothering anybody. This place is dead. There's no one else here besides Melvin and me. And he's dozing off."

I searched for the source and realized it was coming from the booth next to me, the same place I'd heard snoring coming from earlier.

"Oh no, Sheila, I'm doing much, *much* better now. We both had the flu last week. Thank God, we have two bathrooms, if you know what I mean. We could've used two more, though, because it was coming out both ends. And both ends times two people equals four ends. Am I getting too graphic? . . . Oh good. You're absolutely right. What are friends for? Anyway, when I was sitting there in the bathroom, you know *my* bathroom—the purple one with ducks wearing bonnets—I heard Melvin say, 'Hey, Eleanor! I need some more TP in here.' So I says, 'Do I look like Mrs. Whipple? Get your own damn toilet paper!'

"I'm telling you, though, Sheila, getting my sphincter clipped was the best thing I've ever had done!"

Huh?

At that point, my curiosity went into major overdrive. *I have to see what this woman looks like! I've never seen anyone with a clipped sphincter before—that I know of anyway.* I put my fork down and scooted out of my booth, making a squeaking noise against the vinyl seat. As I headed for the restroom and passed by Eleanor's table, I heard her say, "Oh, I *thought* we were alone, but I guess we're not. Someone's been eavesdropping the whole time. The nerve of some people! Honestly! Don't they have anything better to do?"

Like eat a meal in peace without having to hear about your bowel movements and clipped sphincter?

Eleanor, a tiny, impeccably dressed, blue-haired lady, wasn't sitting on an inflatable doughnut as I thought someone with a clipped sphincter might be. And Melvin, who was sound asleep with his mouth agape, was probably making more racket than the instrument used to clip his wife's sphincter.

Eleanor glared at me as I made my way to the restroom. "Oh, Sheila, what has this world come to? You can't even have a nice conversation without nosy people listening in. It's disgraceful."

Another time, I was standing at a urinal in the bathroom at O'Hare Airport, when the ringing of a phone drowned out the sounds of whizzing, spitting, flushing, and Muzak.

"No, I'm at the airport right now. No, no . . . I can talk. I'm just having a bite to eat. Hey, I have that phone number you needed. Can you hold on a sec? Let me put down my hot dog and grab my sack."

Say what?

I got light-headed trying to use my peripheral vision to see what was going on at the next urinal. Sure enough, he'd placed a hot dog on top of the urinal and was simultaneously rummaging through his knapsack while he peed, balancing the phone in the crook of his neck.

Now that takes talent.

"Okay, I think I found it. Yep, here's the card. Just a sec . . . I need another hand," he laughed.

Don't look at me, I thought to myself.

For the next thirty seconds, he talked and peed while I eyed his wienie and wondered what kind of germs were breeding on it. There was nothing more than a flimsy napkin between it and the porcelain. I'd actually finished my own business but couldn't take my eyes off this one-man show.

This guy is amazing, I thought, *but also disgusting*. He ended his phone conversation and ate the rest of his hot dog while zipping up his pants. The only thing he forgot to do before exiting the restroom was wash his hands.

And, yet another time, after an extremely long and exhausting flight from Tokyo to Chicago, I opted to take the three-hour bus ride home rather than drive. I was so ready for a nap.

The bus was full. Actually, it was jam-packed, with almost every seat occupied. After finding a seat, I got myself situated. I was just happy to be off my feet after a busy twelve-hour flight. Just as I started to relax, a large man with ten or fifteen gold chains around his neck squeezed down the aisle and took the seat across the aisle from me. He was a white version of Mr. T.

Soon after, the bus left the terminal. As we inched onto the busy interstate, my eyes got heavier, and I began to drift off. Suddenly, I was almost rocketed to my feet by a sound not unlike a bullhorn. Turns out it was someone's ringtone.

"Hey, bro! No, dude, I can hear you. Can you hear me? No, I said, 'Can you hear me?' CAN YOU HEAR ME?"

We *all* heard him. Helen Keller could've heard him.

"Yo, dude, you're not gonna fuckin' believe this! I just won over thirty-four hundred bucks! No, man, playin' blackjack in Vegas. No, three thousand, four-hundred, and sixty-eight *fuckin'* dollars! Nah, I've got it right here in my pocket in tens and twenties. They said I was nuts for takin' it that way, said I'd probably get knocked off by some asshole. But I figure, how's anyone even gonna know I have it? You know what I'm sayin'? Dude, can you believe it? Almost thirty-five hundred fuckin' dollars—right here in my pocket! Man, are we gonna have us a good time tonight."

For the next hour, seventy-two of us were fortunate enough to hear exactly how Mr. T was going to blow his wad. Although we were forced to listen, not one of us was interested—except perhaps the wild-eyed, yet attentive, crackhead sitting two rows behind him. I had a feeling he could *really* put that thirty-four hundred dollars to good use.

I used to think I preferred texting over voice conversations, but now I'm unsure. When my niece was fourteen, she and her friend came to visit, and during the entire week they were with me, I don't think the two of them uttered more than ten words. They did, however, text *constantly*. Their fingers must've been absolutely exhausted. No matter where we were or what we were doing, they were deeply involved in cyber conversations. Being of a nosy nature, I sometimes peeked over their shoulders to see what they were typing. Oftentimes, the thought-provoking incoming messages required equally thought-provoking responses, like "k," "lmao," and "bcuz."

In six days, the only thing I heard coming from them was *TAP, TAP, TAPPITY TAP.* Finally, on their last day with me, I decided to try a new approach. I fought fire with fire and typed out the following:

"ey! gud AM! s'up? RU awake yet? wadya wn2do 2day? wn2go 2 d bch? wn2 C a moV? mayB go bowlin? or jst stay hre n sit by d p%l? im *vin, so ltz e@ 1st. im hngry nuf 2 e@ a orse. whr DY wn2 e@? u pik. mcDs? bk? tco bel? isn't dis 2 QL dat I knw hw 2 txt now? i tlk lk yr bst pal nt yr uncL, ryt?"

Within seconds of hitting SEND, the girls came bounding down the stairs and into the kitchen.

"Did you get my text?" I asked.

"Uh, yeah."

"Well, why didn't you text me back?" I said with a pouty face.

My niece rolled her eyes. "Uh, that's okay. Let's go do something, okay?"

I never saw either of their phones the rest of that day.

Although I've lived more years without a cell phone than with one, I barely remember what it was like before I had one. I admittedly use mine a lot, but I really do try to keep my conversations somewhat on the private side. And I do even text on occasion. But that's usually when a short message needs to be relayed quickly. I save anything longer for an actual chat . . . as in two voices talking.

But it would be a sheer nightmare if phone usage were allowed during commercial flights. It's bad enough that they're allowed during the boarding process. Passengers come on the airplane, phone to ear, totally ignoring the flight attendant at the entry door.

"Good afternoon. May I help you find your seat?"

No response. Nothing. Nada. Not even a nod to acknowledge that they see you standing there. I've almost been knocked over when the bag precariously perched over the shoulder of the arm whose hand is attached to the phone comes flying down. And still, no comment. No "I'm sorry" or "Excuse me." Just a simple, "Shit."

I especially love it when I'm passing out beverages in first class during boarding, and I have to mouth the words to the idiot who's yapping on his phone. He simply gestures with a wave of the hand for no or a quick point for yes. Very polite.

The simple PA announcement: "At this time, we ask that you turn off and put away all electronic devices" seems clear to me, but for some reason, it can be especially confusing to otherwise intelligent people. They seem to hear their own silent addendum: "that is, except for those using cell phones."

I'm not talking about just passengers either. There are crew members who can be just as bad. God forbid there's ever a medical emergency—unless, of course, you have Nancy's personal number. Yes, she has much more important issues going on at home. She's on the phone with her babysitter, who's complaining that the kids want to stay up past their bedtime. And can they have popcorn at this hour? Thank God Nancy has unlimited minutes!

Yet some people still want to permit the usage of cell phones during flights. *Are they nuts?* They must be, and that's exactly why I signed the petition and try to spread the word. I'm also going to contact my state representatives and give them a piece of my mind—right after I take this incoming call.

In Stitches

I n a seven-month period in 2021, I had nine basal cell carcino-
mas chopped off. That totals over sixty in a twenty-year span.
I seem to have become a basal cell farm, harvesting a bumper
crop in 2021 alone. A good friend discovered the very first one in
2001, when she noticed a small spot on my neck and asked how
long it had been there.

"Oh, a couple of months, I guess." I wasn't really that concerned.

"I had a similar one that turned out to be cancer," she said.
"Promise me you'll make an appointment with a dermatologist."

I half-promised that I would.

As a fair-skinned child who grew up long before sunscreen
was ubiquitous, I was always getting sunburns, mostly on my
face, back, and chest. When I was four years old, I had a burn so
severe on the back of my neck that I suffered convulsions.

Later, as an adolescent and young teen, I often went to the
"dunes" on Lake Michigan, where I'd slather on some Coppertone
then promptly go swimming and wash it all off. After almost
every trip there, I returned home with a blistering sunburn.

Once I reached high school, all the cool kids had good
tans—the darker, the better. And Hollywood really glamorized

it. Everyone wanted to look like George Hamilton or Cher. Me especially. I wanted to be a combination of them both.

Despite my fair skin tone and propensity to burn, I was determined to get a tan. So every summer, I would stupidly cover myself with a mixture of baby oil and iodine, throw a blanket on the grass, and sizzle for a couple hours when the sun was at its highest point. After burning a few times and ruining my skin sufficiently, I would darken a bit. It was a pinkish dark, but it was better than pasty white. One year I added Sun In to the mix in hopes of looking like a surfer, but instead I spent the next four months looking like an orangutan.

After starting my career as a flight attendant, I loved going to all the beach destinations, especially Acapulco. Most of the crew members flying those routes were also beach lovers, so upon arrival, we'd run to our rooms, don our bathing suits, and meet on the beach in minutes, lest we lose any precious sun time. There we would grease up, fill our margarita glasses, and bask in the sun for hours. Our return flight the following day was always in the afternoon, so we'd head back to the beach in the morning to repeat the previous day's activities, sans margaritas. I did this for years.

In March of 1982, I met Rich through a mutual friend. I was immediately enamored by his GQ looks. He was blond, lean, and tan, with piercing blue eyes. Add a pink Polo sweater and tight Calvin Klein jeans, and I was definitely smitten. Our relationship took off quickly. By May, I wanted him to meet my mother, who was living in Florida at the time. We spent ten days there and, except for the small area covered by our Speedos, proudly came home with the best tans we'd ever had. From then on, our favorite vacations were sun- and beach-related, with our destinations of choice being Hawaii and Florida.

While at home in the summer, a hot, sunny day wasn't complete unless we'd gotten a few rays. During the winter months, God forbid we weren't golden brown at all times, so we bought tanning bed memberships. Of course, in those days, the "experts"—who were undoubtedly the manufacturers of the tanning beds—claimed they were safer than the sun's UV rays.

But all that changed for me with a little red spot on my neck. At my first dermatologist visit, a small area was sliced off for a biopsy. Two weeks and six stitches later, the doctor gave me several pamphlets on actinic keratosis, basal cell carcinoma, squamous cell carcinoma, and melanoma, no doubt hoping to scare some sense into me. It certainly caught my attention, but that was about it—until a few months later when I went in for a full screening. During that visit, three spots on my chest were biopsied, and a few days later, the nurse called to say they were indeed basal cell carcinoma and needed to be removed.

Because the three spots were quite small, I naively assumed the incisions would be small, like the one on my neck. And since the appointment was scheduled for early in the morning, I figured I could be out lounging poolside by noon. *Not bad*, I thought.

But bad it was. Of course, I didn't know the extent of it until I got home and ignored the instructions that read, "Do not remove dressing for 24 hours." I carefully peeled off the bandages, then stood looking in the mirror for several minutes as the shock settled in. There were three incisions—each about eight inches long— that had been closed with metal staples, not stitches. I started to count, then recounted. There were *thirty-six* staples in all. It looked like I had crisscrossing train tracks on my once barren chest.

I called out to Rich, wondering where he was since I hadn't seen him when I got home. No answer. I walked out to the kitchen and saw through the window that he was perched on a chaise lounge next to the pool. I walked out, and before I could even say anything, he looked up at me and said, "You look really pale. You gonna come lay out?"

That snapped me right out of my shock. "I would," I replied, feeling my normal, sarcastic self return. "But I have *such* a dilemma." He stared at me blankly, so I continued. "Do I wear my bandages and risk having tan lines, or do I keep them off so I don't have any unsightly lines?" For effect, I lifted my shirt.

With the sun in his eyes, he didn't see the gleaming staples at first. "Why do you have to use that Pauley sarcasm on me?"

Because I like to use my God-given gift, I thought but didn't say. Instead, because I still wanted his sympathy, I said with a fake but realistic quiver in my voice, "She cut me. She cut me real bad."

A few years later, I saw an article in a very respected science magazine about a twenty-year study to examine why such a high percentage of female pilots and flight attendants were getting breast cancer and so many male pilots and flight attendants were getting skin cancer. The article went on to say that during a flight from New York to Paris, which is relatively short for an international flight, the amount of radiation was measured. Surprisingly, it was equivalent to the amount received in several chest X-rays. Depending on the duration of the flights and the destinations flown, radiation levels could be substantially higher. Add ozone levels and thin-skinned planes (to lessen the weight and reduce fuel costs) and the amount of radiation those in my line of work are exposed to could be considerable.

I printed the report and took it to my next screening. I had recently changed dermatologists, mostly because my gut was telling me to. It was a good thing I did because the new doctor found two aggressive cancers that the previous doctor had pooh-poohed each time I'd pointed them out. I left a copy of the report with him, and when I returned the following week to have the two new cancers removed, he told me he'd read the article and couldn't agree more. He felt that in my case, it was probably a combination of a lifetime of sun-worshipping and radiation exposure from my years of flying.

A few years ago, while working a return trip from New Delhi, I told one of my coworkers about my history with skin cancer, and she shared that her husband had also had several removed. Reaching into her purse, she pulled out a small sachet and handed it to me.

"You should try this," she said. "It works really well."

I read the label as she added, "But get it in India. It's a lot cheaper there."

It was a topical cream created initially to eradicate, of all things, genital warts. But, for reasons unknown, someone figured out that it was very effective at destroying basal cell carcinoma as well.

When I got home, I started googling, and sure enough, there were hundreds of positive reviews on its effectiveness. It was said to attack any atypical cells in the region where it was applied.

While my dermatologist was scanning my body during my next screening, he paused at my chest and touched a couple of areas. Then he gently scraped them. After checking the rest of my body, he returned to the two spots. I knew what that meant. He asked if I preferred to have them excised or to have the Mohs method done. The Mohs method involves taking off layer after layer of skin, then examining it under a microscope. It can take minutes or hours, depending on what's found. It's very effective, in that, by studying the skin under a microscope, it determines when the entire cancer margin has been removed, so no biopsy or further care is needed. You just have to let the area—or, in my case from an earlier Mohs procedure, *crater*—heal.

Instead of either of those procedures, however, I pulled out the sachet from my pocket, held it up, and said, "Do you mind if I try this?"

The dermatologist seemed surprised when he saw it. "Really?" he said. "Uh, are you sure?"

Initially I thought he was thinking that I, a mere layman, must have a vast knowledge of all things medically and pharmaceutically related. But I later realized he wasn't thinking that at all. Plus, he must've gone a step further than I had and read the negative reviews as well.

He told me some of the side effects associated with this treatment and explained that it could be rather aggressive in its "attack" on the suspicious areas. He even mentioned that it had a chemo agent in it, which could make me feel quite sick. Unfortunately, I didn't really listen to any of this because I already knew I wanted to try it rather than getting cut again.

For purposes of this story, I'll call this cream, Idareyou. The prescribed usage was to apply it directly to the two small spots on my chest, and apparently, the cream knew what to do from there. I simply had to apply it daily for two weeks, take one week off, then do it for another two weeks. The timing was perfect because I had six weeks off work starting the following month.

In my feeble, unsuspecting mind, I assumed I could still enjoy my vacation. All I really had to do was apply the Idareyou once a day. *Easy peasy*, I thought.

Within two days of starting the regimen, I knew I had assumed wrong. Even though I was only applying it to the two tiny spots, by day two, my entire chest was starting to look angry. By day three, it was even angrier, and by day four, it was downright pissed. Layer after layer of skin had already started sloughing off, and by this point, my entire chest was weeping. I decided to do some more googling, and this time, I scrolled past all the positive reviews I'd previously read.

Ruh-roh.

At that point, I understood why Idareyou was so effective. Formulated to obliterate anything of a suspicious nature, it was clearly doing its job—but at my expense. By the evening of the fourth day, I was wondering if I should start looking for a cemetery plot. But I decided I'd just have to leave that up to Rich because I couldn't even get out of bed.

Looking back, I may have been going in and out of consciousness. I can barely recollect getting out of bed each morning to apply what I imagine felt like battery acid on an open wound. I spent every day in bed with a fever, chills, and body aches. And I couldn't get enough sleep. Rich came home for lunch one day and later told me he thought I was dead. Despite an outdoor temperature of 104 degrees, I had somehow made my way to the thermostat and turned the air conditioner off. Then I put on flannel pajamas, donned a hat, gloves, and a scarf, and added a thick quilt to the bed. When Rich entered the bedroom, I was lying on my back, pale, with my eyes closed and my gloved hands folded on top of my chest.

On day eleven, my chest no longer looked just pissed, it looked like raw hamburger. By the thirteenth day, I realized my nipples were gone. But, despite feeling horrible physically, by day fourteen, I was in a good frame of mind because I knew I was getting a week off from this purgatory.

I've always been a firm believer of the power of positive thinking. So each day, as I began to feel a little better and my hamburger chest began to heal, I decided that I'd go into my next round with nothing but optimism and positive affirmations.

"Idareyou is my friend and is cleansing my body of cancer."

"I will sprout new nipples and be whole again."

"My body will feel no pain or side effects."

On day twenty-two, I started applying Idareyou again. Despite my positive mantras and thoughts, by the end of that week, I felt worse than I did at the end of my first round. I finally caved and called the dermatologist and told him I felt like I was ICU material. He asked if I was capable of driving myself to his office. Being very independent and somewhat of a martyr, I did. When he looked at my chest, he said, "Oh my God, Jim! Stop the Idareyou immediately!"

Upon further examination, he determined that I had a severe staph infection, so he put me on strong antibiotics. Deep down, I was kind of glad, although I worried that having cut the treatment short, it might not have worked its "magic." But once healed, my shiny pink chest—complete with brand spanking new nipples— was cancer-free.

The dermatologist took a picture of my chest that day. It went into my six-inch-thick chart, and every time he had a new nurse or assistant during one of my screenings, he asked that they check out the eight-by-ten-inch photo. They always gave the same shocked reaction: "Wow!"

I'd point my finger at the doctor and deliver my much-rehearsed response, "He did that to me."

Then he'd smile and say, "Well, you asked for it!"

I should've learned my lesson, but during a later screening, the doctor suggested that I use a topical cream on my face for several suspicious spots. He promised that it didn't have a chemo agent like the Idareyou, so I reluctantly agreed to do it on my next four-week-long vacation. Two weeks into the application and several layers of skin later, I felt fine, other than the discomfort of having a face that looked like a pepperoni pizza. After the last application, it healed well. Before I knew it, my face looked just like a baby's behind.

Over the years, on the extremely rare occasion that someone mistakenly tells me that I look younger than I am, Rich always pipes in. "Well, he *should* after all the cosmetic work he's had done!"

Cosmetic work, my ass! I literally lost my face—not to mention my chest, nipples, and dignity—to eradicate those little bastards!

Recently, a very forthright woman I know well told me that I looked pasty. "Get some color, dude!" she advised.

I looked her right in her very wrinkled face—the result of too many years of sun worship and cigarette smoking—smiled, and sweetly quipped, "I know, *I* know. But after dozens and dozens of basal cell, squamous cell, and melanoma cancers, I think I'll just stick with pasty, thank you very much."

Love Always

When I RSVP'd 'yes' to the wedding of an acquaintance's daughter in the summer of 2004, I truly had no idea what I was getting myself into. I really should have since I'd known Karen for almost twenty-six years. But then again, I hadn't actually seen her in close to twenty-five. Our friendship was a long-distance one, based mostly on letters we sent to each other and the occasional phone call.

When I started my career as a flight attendant in the winter of 1978, Dallas was my first base. Not knowing a soul there, I rather hastily found an apartment and signed a six-month lease. It was just before Christmas, and being on call, I was gone a lot. And because I was rarely home, I really didn't have the time or energy to meet people and make new friends.

One day, I was washing my clothes in the small laundry room of my two-star apartment complex. Thinking I was alone as I unloaded the washing machine, I almost dropped my armful of damp clothes when someone screamed, "Hey, you seen my underwear?"

I turned around, and a short, plump lady was standing there. As she stuck her head into the other washer, she echoed into the drum, "Where are my damn underwear? You got them in *your* clothes?" As I searched my own unmentionables, sure enough, there they were, wound tightly around several pairs of my briefs. Although it should've been a somewhat embarrassing moment, she seemed unfazed. Grabbing her bloomers out of my hand and heading to the door, she turned and said, "Thanks! Hey, I'm Karen. Who are you?" I had just made a new friend.

Karen starting popping in whenever I was in town. And since she didn't work, she popped in a *lot*. We really didn't seem to have much in common, but I found her to be very entertaining. She also had a bawdy sense of humor, which bordered on being downright dirty, so we did share that common bond.

She was especially good at popping in around mealtimes— breakfast, lunch, dinner, or all three. And she also became really good at borrowing things and not returning them.

She had moved to Dallas from Ohio with her boyfriend, Danny, two months before I arrived. They had only known each other for a couple of weeks when he told her he was moving to Dallas. She saw that as an opportunity to better her life, so she gave him a sloppy blow job, told him she loved him, packed her bags, and headed to the Bid D.

"He's kind of an asshole, but he's making good money, Jim," she told me over rum and Cokes one night. "And I'm not giving that up!"

In the several months I lived there, I never met Danny. He was always working. But Karen kept me informed of what was going on in their lives. She seemed happy as long as he worked long hours and paid the bills, which allowed her to stay at home, lose her underwear, and mooch off me.

After nine months in Dallas, I started feeling homesick, so

I put my transfer in for Chicago. It was approved, and I moved there in September. One day, the phone rang, and when I answered, the operator asked if I would accept a collect call from Karen. I figured something must be wrong.

"That motherfucker kicked my ass out!" she screamed into the phone. "Said I was lazy and that I was usin' him! Can you believe that, Jim?"

I could believe that.

"Where are you living?" I asked.

"I'm stayin' with my cousin in Fort Worth," she said matter-of-factly. "He's not chargin' me rent since I'm not workin'."

A few weeks later, Karen called again—collect, of course.

"Hel——?" I tried.

"I'm *pregnant!*" she interrupted.

Surprised but not surprised, I said, "Oh, I didn't realize you're dating someone."

"Datin' someone? I'm not."

I figured since I was already involved in this, I might as well go a little deeper. "Who's the father?"

"I don't know," she replied casually. "I met these three guys at 7-Eleven when I went in for a Big Gulp. Two of 'em were Mexicans and the other was a Uranian or something like that."

At that point, it was getting interesting, so I urged her on.

"So I took 'em back to the apartment. Anyway, they were gettin' all frisky—'specially after I lifted my blouse—so the four of us had some fun, if you know what I mean."

I had a good idea what she meant, but I desperately tried *not* to visualize her with her blouse lifted. She said she ended up "makin' love" with all of them. *Gang bang* was actually the term that came to my mind.

"Can you believe I'm gonna be a mama, Jim? I hope it's a boy, and I hope he looks just like his daddy. I kinda hope it's the Uranian. Damn! I get all moist down there just thinkin' about him! 'Course if he is the daddy, I don't even know how to get ahold of him. Maybe I'll see him again when I go in for a Big Gulp."

I couldn't help but ask, "When you say 'Uranian,' do you mean *I*ranian? Or is he from Uranus?"

"From my *what?*" she asked, clearly confused. But then, as it dawned on her, she bellowed into my previously undamaged ear. "God dammit, Jim! You know what I mean. He's from Uran. You know . . . one of those dark, handsome, foreign guys with a really big . . . well, let's just say he filled me up, if you know what I mean."

Again, I did.

Over the next few months, Karen kept me informed, mostly by letters, of how her pregnancy was going. And then, in early January, I received an envelope containing a Polaroid snapshot with a handwritten note stating that little Thomas had made his debut. It also read, "Congratulations, Uncle Jim!"

As I studied the photo, it appeared that Thomas might've been more Uranian—I mean Iranian—than Mexican, so I knew Karen was happy.

Meanwhile, I was acclimating well to my new life in Chicago. I was flying great destinations, meeting new people, and enjoying life in the city. During one of my telephone conversations with Karen, I tried to tell her this. She couldn't have cared less, though, mostly because it wasn't about her.

At the beginning of February, I received a letter from Karen. With poor punctuation, bad grammar, and numerous misspellings, she wrote:

Dear Jim,

Want is new? My birthday is in three week. Can you belief it? Yes, februry 13 is my birthday and Ill be 22 years old. And I'm a mother. A mother Jim! To the best of my ebilly, I'm rising Thomas to be a good man who well always love and take care of me. So I decided to move back to Ohio Jim. I din't know want else to due. I'm living with my mother, and she's not chargin me rent. But guess what Jim. I met Mr. Rite. His name is Billy and he works at a dirty book store. He's actually the manger. And you know want, Jim. He was gay until he met me, but I turned him round. Were gittin married.

Ill make sure to send you some pitchers once I get flim for my camera.

ps Don't forget my birthday is februry 13.
Hey, can you loan me $50?

Love always,
Karen

And pitchers she sent! When I saw Billy, I wondered how in the world he could've possibly ever been gay. He had greasy, long hair, a shaggy, untrimmed beard, and an overall unkempt appearance. In one photo, he had his arm draped around Karen, with his long, dirty talons resting on her shoulder. It looked like he needed to go through a car wash—perhaps twice.

Over the next few years, I continued to hear from Karen. She shared stories of her life with Thomas, Billy, and the two daughters that came along after they married. Maybe she really had turned Billy around. Or maybe she just frequented a nearby 7-Eleven.

As the years progressed, I always got a letter at the beginning of February to remind me of her upcoming birthday. She also kept me informed about their lives. Thomas and the girls were growing by leaps and pounds, Billy quit his job at the dirty book-store and became a truck driver, and Karen continued her own job as a stay-at-home mom and money manager.

When the youngest was ten, Karen and Billy abruptly packed their bags and moved the family to Texas. Billy quit his job as a truck driver and took a job at a Kmart just a block from the house they rented.

As the three children became teenagers, they all took jobs at the same Kmart. I'm pretty certain they all surrendered their weekly paychecks to Karen, while she screeched, "Mama needs those checks to pay the bills!"

About eight years into their stint in Texas, I received an enve-lope from Karen that was much larger than the ones she typically sent. Inside was a letter and an invitation. Her oldest daughter, Mindy, was getting married, and I was invited. I asked Rich if he wanted to go, but he declined and asked his usual question, "Why do you stay friends with her? She's a user!"

As I'd explained to him before, I said that because she'd been in my life for so many years, I felt she and I had some sort of connection, albeit a majorly dysfunctional one. True, her letters and our phone calls were *all* about her own sordid life, and she rarely, if ever, asked about me. Not once had I received a birthday card from her, more than likely because she had no idea when my birthday was. Nevertheless, I tried to reason with myself that underneath it all, she was probably a good person. And she did have an entrepreneurial nature, although it only involved someone else's hard work and money. Or maybe it was just the fact that I looked forward to getting her letters because they were always amusing.

I decided to go to the wedding.

When I called Karen to tell her, she immediately asked, "Are you rentin' a car? Be sure and get a really big one, okay?" Always thinking ahead, that girl.

When I made my car rental reservation, however, I purposely requested a subcompact. And when I googled different hotels, I chose the one that was farthest away from the church and requested only one bed. I didn't want to take any chances of having an overnight guest . . . or five.

On the day I arrived in Dallas, I picked up my luggage and went to the car rental terminal. The very nice young lady waiting on me smiled and said, "Why sir, this is y'all's lucky day! Y'all got an upgrade to a full-size sedan!"

"Oh, thank you, but I prefer a subcompact."

"You *what?*" She was clearly surprised.

"I appreciate it, but I want the smallest car available. Do you have any Mini Coopers?"

"No," she answered as she looked at the screen. "But we do have a Mazda Miata available. However, it's considered a sports car, so it's fifty dollars extra per day."

"I'll take it!"

A few minutes later, I zoom-zoomed out of the parking lot and headed to the hotel. Once situated and unpacked, I called Karen.

"We're at the church, decoratin' the fellowship hall for the reception." She gave me the address before adding, "The rehearsal will start at six, then we're goin' to Cracker Barrel for dinner."

I was beside myself. Now, I've been invited to several rehearsal dinners over the years, but none so fancy as one at a Cracker Barrel. I hoped I wasn't underdressed.

When I arrived at the church and entered the fellowship hall, I suddenly heard what sounded like a bullhorn. "Jesus Christ! Is that you, Jim?"

I scanned the room to find where the sound had come from just in time to see Karen begin rocking her short, wide frame in an attempt to get out of her chair. With one last grunt, she pulled the chair off her ass and made her way toward me. We hugged each other before she stood back and yelled, "Ever'one, this is my *best friend*, Jim!"

I was introduced to her three children, whom I'd never actually met before. And although I'd never even spoken to them prior to that moment, they all said I was their "favorite uncle." Of course, I'd seen pictures of them throughout the years, though. Thomas, the oldest, had grown into . . . well, let's just say that Thomas had definitely grown. His younger sisters had too. Mindy, the bride-to-be, introduced me to her fiancé, Eric, who looked to be about eighteen, stood well over six feet tall, and weighed about eighty pounds. The youngest daughter, Tina Sue, who was barely seventeen, struck a provocative pose and said, "Ooh, I bet I could turn you straight, Uncle Jim!"

Out of nowhere, a good-looking young man suddenly appeared and hissed at Tina Sue with a sneer, "Back off, bitch!"

Her shoulders slumped as she lifted his arm and crawled underneath. His name was Mark, and I later found out that he lived with the family in a three-bedroom bungalow.

I helped with the decorating until about six, at which time we all herded upstairs to the tiny church sanctuary. Karen, the self-proclaimed matriarch-in-charge, continued barking orders, although her expletive usage had diminished considerably since there was a clergyman present.

As the rehearsal began, everyone took their places. The minister began giving directions, or at least tried to do so. Karen sat in the front pew, repeating everything he said only several decibels louder.

Once the bride and the three couples in the wedding party were lined up and ready to walk down the aisle, Karen turned and yelled, "Turn the cassette on!"

Elvis's "Love Me Tender" soon filled the small church and everyone turned around. Mindy entered on the arm of a homeless man, who I quickly ascertained was Billy, her previously gay, now straight father.

As they made their way down the aisle, Karen started blubbering, "I can't believe my little girl's gettin' married! Mama ain't never been prouder, baby girl."

After the vows were recited, the rehearsal ended. But no sooner had it ended when the screaming began. "Whaddaya mean you didn't pick up your check today? How the *hell* are we supposed to pay for dinner?"

Billy mumbled that he had simply forgotten to run by Kmart and pick up his paycheck.

Karen continued screaming and berating him until Thomas suggested, "I've got twenty bucks. Let's just get pizza."

Feeling a bit guilty and not wanting to appear like a mooch during this momentous occasion, I offered another twenty. We were all back in the fellowship hall when Thomas arrived half an hour later with four large pizzas.

After devouring our delicious meal, the minister asked if he could lock up. As we all headed to the door, Karen hollered, "I'm ridin' with my best friend, Jim! And no one else is!"

Once we squeezed into the small car, I put it in drive and headed out of the parking lot. Before we even got to the street, Karen looked at me and said, "He don't want me no more, Jim."

"He don't?" I asked, trying to sound sincere. I assumed she was talking about Billy.

"No, he don't. We try every Sunday, but he just can't get it up. And I have needs, Jim, you know what I mean? So I found me this Mexican, and we've been gettin' it on. Actually, I found me two Mexicans."

I wasn't sure how to respond, so I asked, "Where did you find them?"

"I was gettin' the mail one day, and they were comin' out of the gun shop next door."

"Do you get a hotel room?" I should've known better than to ask.

"No, one of 'em has a flatbed truck, so we've been doin' it there."

With the visual of the three of them in the back of a flatbed truck, I was afraid to ask any more questions. But I didn't need to because Karen just continued anyway.

"I think Billy turned gay again. You know why I think that, Jim? Because I caught him givin' Mark a blow job, that's why."

"Wait . . . what? You mean Tina Sue's boyfriend, Mark?"

"Yeah, turns out Billy was gettin' him drunk just so he could give him blow jobs. I ain't about to tell Tina Sue, though. It would just tear her up."

I couldn't speak from personal experience, but I totally understood. It's not a good thing to find out your father is giving your boyfriend head.

As we drove along, Karen gave me directions to her house. "Once you see the huge sign that says, 'Load 'Em Up Gun and Ammo Shop,' it's right next door."

As I continued on, I saw the sign, which in the north we call a billboard. I guess everything really is bigger in Texas. Pulling up to the house, I asked where I should park since the whole front yard was already full of vehicles, most of which were resting on cement blocks.

After helping Karen out of the car, we started walking toward the small house. The front door was wide open, and loud voices could be heard. Then the smell hit me. It was actually more of a stench—a really, really *bad* stench. I wondered if someone had forgotten to take out the garbage. But once I got inside, I realized that not only did they forget to take out the garbage, they'd also forgotten to bag it and, instead, had just thrown it on the floor.

"Well, Jim, this here's my house!"

As we entered, two chihuahuas ran toward us, barking and snarling wildly, and one started nipping at my ankles. We continued into the squalor, aka the living room, as I shook Cujo off my pant leg. Just then, Karen screamed louder than I've ever heard anyone scream, "Who the HELL has been sittin' in Mama's chair? *NO ONE* sits in Mama's chair!"

Mama's chair, it turned out, was a new recliner lift chair. It was in the mid-lift position, with little legs sticking out. From deep inside the seat cushion, a small child's voice rang out, "It's me, Aunt Karen."

"Now, *dammit*, Makaylia, you know better than to sit in my chair!"

The little girl hopped down and scurried out the door.

"Ain't nobody else better be thinkin' of sittin' in Mama's chair!" Karen screeched. Then in a quiet, almost sweet voice, she asked, "What do you think of my house, Jim?"

"Very cozy," I lied, wondering how I could make a speedy exit and return to the relaxing confines of my hotel room.

Just then, Thomas bounded into the room with a beer in each hand. "Look what I got! I wanna get shit-faced with my favorite uncle!" he exclaimed as he motioned for me to sit down.

As I considered my options, the ratty sofa appeared to be the best bet, and the middle cushion seemed the least stained, so I sat there. But all of a sudden, I was propelled about a foot into the air when Thomas and Mindy plopped down on either side of me. When I finally landed back on the cushion, I was still several inches above them. They both draped an arm around my shoulders, and Thomas downed the first of many beers.

Just then, Cujo's sister, who seemed a little nicer, jumped on my lap. As I lifted my hand for her to smell, she started growling. Then she bared her teeth, snarling and hacking simultaneously.

"Aw, Angel has a new friend," Karen remarked as the overworked motor of her chair lowered her.

"Uh . . . I don't think she likes me," I commented, very slowly retracting my hand.

At the same time, a rather attractive young lady appeared. I'd seen her at the rehearsal but hadn't met her. She walked toward me and said, "No, that's not her 'I don't like you' growl."

Then she leaned over and stuck her face within inches of Angel's. Without saying a word, she simply stared at the dog.

Angel went ballistic, growling and snarling viciously with her teeth bared and spittle flying everywhere. That lasted for what seemed like half an hour, and all the while, the little dog was still sitting on my lap.

Finally, the young woman stood up and said, "That's her 'I don't like you' growl."

As she walked away, I asked my "nephew and niece" who she was. Thomas was busy guzzling his third beer, so Mindy answered, "Oh, that's Tina Sue's boyfriend's sister, Tammy. She lives here too."

Angel, who was still on my lap, had relaxed a bit after her standoff with Tammy. But then she looked back at me and started to growl and snarl all over again—only this time her tail was wagging.

I finally said I had to call it a night, partly because I was exhausted, partly because I wanted to take a twenty-minute scalding hot shower back at my hotel, and partly because Thomas had barfed over the arm of the couch and Karen was harping on him to clean it up.

The next morning, after a good night's sleep, I phoned Karen.

"Oh, Tammy's doin' our hair and makeup, Jim. You ain't gonna recognize me."

Since they were busy, I told her I would just see her at the church for the ceremony at four.

"Get your scrawny ass over here NOW!" she shrieked. "We ain't seen each other in over twenty-five years!"

When I arrived, I knew it was the right house because of the familiar stench. And I didn't even have to knock because the door was still wide open. Angel and Cujo greeted me. Both were growling and barking while wagging their tails frantically. They were as crazy as their humans.

Karen heard the ruckus and made her way into the living room. "What do you think of my new dress, Jim? The kids got it for me at Penney's. It was almost forty dollars."

"Very pretty," I replied, being honest. It actually was a pretty dress. On another person, that is. It was brown satin and sleeveless, with a plunging neckline, and it still had the price tag attached. Suddenly, Karen's alter ego, Cheryl Tiegs, surfaced as she turned around so I could get the full effect. With one last pivot, I asked if she planned on wearing the curlers she had in her hair to the wedding.

"God dammit, Jim! You're always messin' with me!" she guffawed. "And that's why you're my *best* friend!"

Tammy, who was standing in the doorway to the kitchen, said, "We'll work on gettin' that zipped up later."

I looked at my watch. It was a little after nine thirty . . . in Texas . . . in the summer . . . with no air-conditioning because "it broke six months ago." The wedding wasn't scheduled to start for over six hours, so I just assumed Karen would take off the dress for a few hours. Silly me. I assumed wrong—again.

As I sat on my spot in the center of the ratty sofa, I noticed that Thomas's vomit was still there from the day before. It was right next to a big pile of poop that appeared too large to have come out of a chihuahua's little bunghole.

The longer I sat there listening to Karen ordering Tammy to "Make me look beautiful, dammit!" the more I wished I'd stayed in the cleanliness of my hotel room. But that thought quickly vanished when Karen yelled, "Billy, go get me some pantyhose at the Dollar Depot! Get me the biggest ones they have . . . in nude!"

Then she added, "Jim, will you take him? Oh and Billy, you better go to the Five Buck Barn and get yourself a shirt for the weddin'! And a hat if they got one!"

We were soon in the Miata, headed to do our very important last-minute tasks. Out of the corner of my eye, I could see Billy checking me out. Feeling a little nervous, I started babbling. "So . . . you must like it here?" I asked semi-sincerely since I didn't know what else to say.

"Yeah," he mumbled, "I'm likin' it a lot." Then he winked at me and smiled.

Until then, I hadn't really noticed his nicotine-stained mustache or that his few remaining teeth obviously hadn't been brushed for some time. Luckily, we were approaching the Dollar Depot.

As instructed, we bought a pair of extralarge pantyhose in nude, then headed to the Five Buck Barn, where Billy found a defective white dress shirt. Defective in that the already-short sleeves had been cut even shorter. As we walked toward the checkout, he spotted a cheap black gaucho hat and perched it on his head. Although it was about three sizes too small, he now had the perfect ensemble to walk his daughter down the aisle.

When we returned to the house, Karen clomped into the living room, still in her new dress but now curler-free. "These goddamn shoes are killin' me!" she howled loud enough for neighboring counties to hear. I wondered how the poor, goddamn shoes felt. They were nothing more than flat, bejeweled sandals with straps that were stretched to the max. Karen informed us that the minute Mindy and Eric were pronounced husband and wife, the shoes were coming off.

As two o'clock approached, I told them I was heading back to the hotel. Walking to my car, I suddenly realized Billy was about two steps behind me.

"Want me to come with you?" he mumbled, winking at me again.

"Uh, no thanks," I said before hopping into the car and speeding away.

I arrived at the church around three thirty so I wouldn't miss seeing the other guests show up. I took a seat at the end of a pew with a good view of the entryway.

Just a few minutes before four, Karen made her entrance. As she sauntered down the aisle, she looked from side to side, telling everyone, "Sit down and shut up. It's about to start."

After she took her place in the front pew, she turned and mouthed, "Now!" to the person operating the cassette player. Poor quality music soon filled the church as the bridesmaids and groomsmen made their way down the aisle. Then came Tina Sue and Mark, the maid of honor and best man, respectively.

At each pew, Tina Sue, who had decided to improvise rather than follow the script, stopped and struck a provocative pose, perhaps to show off the huge safety pin that was holding up her dress. Once they finally found their masking tape X on the carpet, the music stopped. Then, after the whirring sound of the tape forwarding, Elvis started singing, "Love Me Tender." You could've heard a pin drop. I silently prayed that it wouldn't be Tina Sue's safety pin.

Everyone stood as Mindy and her gaucho-hatted, short sleeve-wearing, gay-turned-straight-turned-gay father walked through the double doors. It was an emotional moment for everyone, especially Karen, who howled, "My baby girl is gettin' married!"

After Mindy and Billy finally arrived at the altar, the minister began a brutally long and boring dissertation. Luckily, the sound of someone's stomach growling in the pew behind me drowned out most of it.

When it was finally over, the new couple French-kissed for five minutes, then we all made our way downstairs to the basement. I'd like to say the reception that followed was one of the most memorable, beautifully decorated, incredibly catered, and fantastically fun receptions that I've ever been to. I'd like to, but I can't. It was definitely memorable, though. And I have to admit that there was plenty of food—after all, the guests had been instructed to bring a dish to pass and a two-liter bottle of pop. There was also something else I'd never seen at a reception: In the middle of the gift table was a huge glass jar with a sign that read, "Honeymoon money. And don't be a cheap ass!" There was already a dollar bill inside, just in case anyone wasn't smart enough to figure it out.

Karen, who had kept her promise and was already bare-foot—with her extralarge nude pantyhose and goddamn shoes tossed to the side—sat near the jar to ensure that no one would steal the money.

After loading up on ham sandwiches, potato salad, baked beans, tortilla chips, nacho cheese, and seventeen different Jell-O salads, people took to the dance floor. Karen, who didn't need a microphone, suddenly screeched, "Get ready, everyone! The five-dollar dance is gonna start! Get in line!"

People reluctantly started lining up as they dug into their pockets, purses, and fanny packs. I overheard a couple of them say, "*Five* dollars?"

Soon it was time for the bouquet and garter toss. A sturdy chair was brought out for Mindy, then Eric slowly lifted her dress, giving those of us unlucky enough to be sitting front and center a view of something we will never, *ever* forget.

As things started to wind down and guests began to leave, I looked over to see Karen sitting with her naked legs splayed wide apart, counting money from the honeymoon jar. As she finished, she screamed, "YEE-HAW!" waving a wad of bills in the air. "We made $107.22!" Everyone cheered and clapped, no doubt imagining what an incredible honeymoon that sum would afford.

Before leaving, I helped take down all the tables and put away the folding chairs, while Karen sat and directed us. As I was saying my goodbyes, she said, "I'm gonna make you breakfast tomorrow, Jim."

Remembering what her kitchen looked like, I told her my flight had changed, and I had to leave at 6:00 a.m. rather than noon. It hadn't, but I can be a good liar when absolutely necessary. And this was absolutely necessary.

Over the next few months, I received several letters from Karen, keeping me informed of all the new happenings. "Eric still wont work." "Tina Sue got herself pregnut." "Mindy brake my damn chair!" "Angel and Cujo had another liter." "Billy is still blown Mark." And, as she always did, she ended her letter by asking:

Hey, think I could have $50?
Love always,
Karen

A couple of years after the wedding, she wrote the following, in all her misspelled, poorly punctuated glory:

That lazy ass Eric still dont want work, so Mindy been working two jobs. Anyway, she asked about tranfering, and kmart tell her she could. She want to go to Indiana so she can live with her faverite uncle. I'll let you know when their moving.

Hey, you got $50?
Love always,
Karen

Later that evening as I read the letter to Rich, I said, "That's strange. I know Karen has a couple of brothers in Ohio, and one lives in Texas now, but she never spoke of a brother in Indiana." Then we looked at each other as it slowly dawned on us. "No, no, no, no, NO! Oh, *hell* no!" I exclaimed.

I quickly wrote a response to Karen, explaining that we had way too much on our plates at the time. Our mothers were both in failing health, and there was a good chance that one or both of them might be coming to stay with us. Plus, unlike Eric, who refused to even look for a job, we were both working a lot. Knowing Karen, I couldn't leave any room for even the possibility of them moving in and mooching off us, so I simply said, "No."

I sent the letter early the next morning, and a few days later, I received a scathing reply lambasting me with misspelled expletives. Suddenly I was a "selfish basturd" who didn't give a "shite" about his "own family." She claimed she hadn't been asking for much, just to let my "niece" stay with me for "a while." Of course, the "niece's" husband would've been freeloading too. Had I said yes, they would probably still be living with us. She also wrote that she now knew what I was capable of and had lost all "trist" in me.

I never responded even though it bothered me a lot. I felt I'd been a good friend to her over the years, but obviously that didn't matter. In her eyes, I had betrayed "my own family."

I've thought about Karen many times since then, wondering where she is and what she's doing. I've also wondered why we remained friends for so long. She was a user from the very beginning. I knew that from the moment I met her, so shame on me for allowing it, I guess. I also knew we had been raised very differently. My parents had instilled values in me as well as a strong work ethic that I've continued to use throughout my life. Whenever I wanted something, I was always told, "Then get your ass out there and work for it!"

Ending a relationship, especially a long-term one, is never easy. But it becomes necessary when it's no longer positive or open to any type of growth—or when the give-and-take simply becomes take. As Karen once said to me, "I have needs, Jim." I understand that completely now. I have needs too. I need friends who support me when I need to be supported, who listen to me when I need to be heard, who hug me when I need to be hugged, who cry with me when I need to cry, and who laugh with me when I need to laugh. I need true friends.

Love always? Yes, but sometimes, for our own good, it's just best to do it from afar.

So Sari

In 2005, when the airline I worked for announced it would be starting nonstop service from Chicago to New Delhi the following month, most of my colleagues couldn't contain their excitement. It had been a long time since we'd gotten a new destination, let alone an exotic one like India. Although I had the seniority to fly the trip, I was on the fence as to whether I should do it in the beginning or wait until all the glitches had been worked out. But when I ran into a coworker one day, she tried talking me out of doing it at all.

"I have a friend with another airline who's done the New York–Mumbai route several times, and she has tons of horror stories!" she warned.

She repeated a few of the stories, but I was undeterred. I wanted to go to India, so I bid to fly the route for a month. I figured if I hated it, it was only one month out of my life, and I would never have to do it again.

As it turned out, I loved it.

On my first trip, which happened to be the day after the inaugural flight, the plane was jam-packed, mostly with Indian nationals. Typically when a new destination is just starting up, the flights are only about half full. This flight was not typical in any way.

Although I pride myself on being open-minded and a bit of a world traveler, I found that I knew very little about the Indian culture. I quickly learned that Indians have little to no concept of personal space. But I'd recently read that the country had the second-largest population in the world, with 1.4 billion inhabitants, including thirty-one million in New Delhi alone. It's no wonder they know nothing about personal space—they don't have any!

With that in mind, on that first flight, several passengers decided the best place to congregate was in our galley. And on a Boeing 777, the galley in the back is huge. There's a reason we refer to it as the ballroom. The passengers, however, weren't using it for dancing. Some were there to visit and make new friends, while others found it to be the perfect yoga studio. We saw a few people with legs extended perpendicular over their heads, while several others meditated in the lotus position on the floor. A few even struck the lion pose, which is a bit unnerving seeing so many mouths agape.

Many were there simply to drink tea—lots and lots of tea. There were even a handful of young mothers who hadn't gotten the memo that breastfeeding should be more of a private moment between the baby and mother. For the most part, though, that went unnoticed—especially when two people decided to change their clothes in the middle of the galley.

Because I was working the galley that day, I felt I should probably try to keep some semblance of order, especially since this was also our work space. Typically the person "working galley" is responsible for setting up all the carts for the food and beverage service, which on this very long flight amounted to no less than three meals plus snacks. It also requires throwing all the chicken and vegetarian entrees into one of several ovens and turning them to 275 degrees for twenty minutes or until you smell something burning. It's enough to make a gourmet chef or even a short-order cook at Denny's wince. However, it didn't make our passengers wince. In fact, it was quite the contrary. The minute I started preparing for the next meal service, an unheard and possibly telepathic invitation seemed to resonate throughout the cabin, "Come back to the galley! Jim needs your company!"

I approached one of the half-naked men standing in the middle of the galley and kindly suggested, "Sir, we have several lavatories if you'd like to change your clothes in private."

He looked up from his important task of zipping his pants, wobbled his head, and said, "I would like some tea." Wobble, wobble. "A hot tea." Wobble. "A veddy, *veddy* hot tea." Wobble, wobble.

Although this was our first flight to India, we quickly discovered that they weren't talking about Lipton tea. We'd been given what seemed like hundreds of bags of masala chai tea mix, initially thinking this was way too much for one flight. It wasn't. We ran out two hours before landing.

We also soon discovered that it was easiest to mix a lot of hot milk and sugar in the pots of tea before throwing them in the ovens that still smelled of burnt chicken and curried vegetables. This alleviated a multitude of requests for individual packets of sugar and gallons of hot milk. Usually. There were still some who wanted ten or eleven packets of sugar in their cup, perhaps to ensure they'd be wide awake for the duration of the sixteen-hour flight so as not to miss any of the excitement in the galley.

Once the main meal was served and the lights were turned off, the other flight attendants and I cleared out the galley as much as we could. We were hoping to finally sit down on one of the very uncomfortable hard plastic boxes used to store the catering items. But that proved to be difficult because several passengers were still hanging around drinking tea in various yoga poses.

Suddenly, our quiet chaos was interrupted when a call light went off—not once but several times. By the number of dings, I assumed the absolute worst. As I sprinted up the aisle to investigate, I made a mental note of where the nearest defibrillator was in case someone was in full cardiac arrest. Once I arrived, I found a family of five sitting comfortably. Still out of breath, I asked, "Yes, do you need something?"

The father was the first to answer. "Yes, I would like a juice," he answered, wobbling his head. No signs of cardiac arrest.

"Would you like apple, mango, orange, or cranberry?"

Wobble, wobble, wobble, wobble. "Mango," he answered. Wobble, wobble.

As a seasoned flight attendant, I knew better than to leave and bring just one glass of juice back to a family of five, so I looked at the mother and asked, "Would you like a mango juice too?"

Wobble, wobble. I took that as a yes.

Next was the oldest son, who was about seven years old and engrossed in his Game Boy.

"Would you like a mango juice?" I asked.

Without even looking up, he wobbled.

I then leaned over the five-year-old and asked her the same question. Wobble, wobble.

I wondered if the youngest, who was perhaps two years old

and hanging on to a sippy cup, would even understand. I gave it a shot. "Would you like me to fill your sippy cup with mango juice?"

I was a bit taken aback when he looked up at me and wobbled his little head enthusiastically.

For the most part, the rest of the flight was uneventful. As I finished up my final tasks and prepared for landing, I couldn't wait to get to my hotel room, take a long, hot shower, and get some much-needed rest. Immediately after the airplane touched down, I made eye contact with another flight attendant who was in his jump seat across the aisle. The strangest odor had suddenly permeated the entire cabin. It was a choking and very dense smoke, something I had never experienced in all my years of flying. He and I were on high alert, wondering what the source of the smoke was.

Before I could wonder too long, the interphones started ringing. It was the purser informing us that the captain had called and told her the smoke smell was normal for India. We found out later that, because it was a somewhat cool seventy-five-degree night, cow dung was being burned for warmth. For those of us who continued to fly this destination, it truly did become the norm.

After we arrived and deplaned, we made our way to the customs hall. Despite what we'd heard, clearing customs was rather quick and organized. It was shortly after midnight when we boarded the bus that would take us to the hotel. Although I was exhausted, I didn't want to miss anything on the ride. Even though it was so late, the traffic was quite heavy, and I saw every mode of transportation imaginable. Cars, trucks, bicycles, buses, motorbikes, and tuk-tuks were going in every direction, honking, and weaving in and out of total mayhem. I looked out of the curtain-and-fringe-laden window next to me at one point and thought I was dreaming. I was eyeball to eyeball with an elephant with a sole rider perched on its back. A few minutes later, a small motor scooter with a family of five stacked on it sped past us. And at one point, I was surprised to see a double-decker bus—until I realized it was just a regular bus that was so packed with people that several of them had climbed onto the roof and were hanging on for dear life.

About an hour into our journey, the bus came to a sudden halt. A cacophony of horn honking erupted while we just sat there. Finally, after about twenty minutes, one of our pilots asked the driver if there was a problem.

"No, sir." Wobble, wobble. "There is just a cow in the road."

Several of us moved forward to have a look. Sure enough, a cow had decided to take a nap in the middle of this busy boulevard. It was the skinniest cow I had ever seen. It looked like the Twiggy version of cows.

When the pilot asked if someone could gently urge it along, this brought a whole lot of wobbling from the driver. "Oh no, sir. We cannot disturb a sacred cow."

I almost asked if I, being a Christian, could give it a swift kick in the rear so we could get to the hotel.

When we finally arrived at the hotel and I got to my room, it was all I could do to unpack and make my nest. Although the plan was to take a long, hot shower, I barely remember undressing and stumbling into bed. The next thing I knew, it was six o'clock in the morning. I lay there a bit, wondering where I was and why I was there. I finally decided to get up and attempt a workout. Although I was still exhausted, I didn't want to chance sleeping too long, then not get a nap in before the long trip home that evening.

As I was leaving the state-of-the-art fitness room in our five-star hotel, I noticed that they offered both Indian and Swedish massages. I inquired about the Indian massage and was told that it was given by two people. In other words, there was a person on either side giving a totally synchronized massage. I decided to give it a whirl because I like to try new things and I love massages.

But first I went back to my room, showered, and headed to breakfast, where I found several of my colleagues raving about the incredible food. I went to the various buffet tables before eating my body weight in the most incredible, colorful cornucopia of delicacies imaginable.

When I arrived at the scheduled time for my massage, Sanjay, one of my massage therapists, greeted me. He took me to the locker room, opened a locker, and asked me to disrobe. Then he just stood there. I waited a moment, then asked, "Like, right now? Should I take off everything?"

"Yes, please, sir," he answered with the slightest of wobbles.

As I had done many times in my life, especially when visiting my proctologist and urologist, I decided to leave my dignity right there and made a mental note to pick it up on my way out. I unbuttoned my shirt and took it off as my audience of one stood there watching me. He took my shirt and hung it neatly on a hanger. Next were the pants, which were also carefully folded and hung. With each article of clothing, my new personal valet folded it with the utmost care. I was especially glad I had put on clean underwear that morning. Not that I would have them on for long. At least Sanjay gave me a towel to get from the locker room to the steam sauna where I was instructed to sit for twelve minutes.

From there, I was led to a tranquil massage room, where I was told to get on the solid wood table. Thankfully, the room had very low lighting and relaxing music. After I was splayed out in all my naked glory, Sanjay's comrade, Manjeet, entered the room. Since I'd already left my dignity behind, I was no longer embarrassed, even when they excitedly started speaking in Hindi. Sanjay spoke very limited English, and Manjeet spoke none. Later I found out that even the most mundane conversations sound exciting when spoken in Hindi, so I shouldn't have flattered myself. I figured it was more than likely that they weren't even talking about the naked American in front of them.

I had requested the Indian Ayurvedic massage as well as the shirodhara therapy, which was recommended by a friend who had visited India years before. All I knew was that it involved oil being dripped on the forehead. Asking Sanjay and Manjeet to explain it in greater detail was fruitless, so I just relaxed and decided to go with the flow.

My eyes were covered with cotton balls to keep out the oil, then a strip of cloth was placed over them and tied around my head. *Why couldn't they have placed a strip of cloth somewhere else?* I wondered, still a bit self-conscious about my nudity. Not being able to see anything helped tremendously, though, especially if they were pointing at certain body parts and laughing.

As the warm and mildly scented oil was drizzled on my forehead, back and forth, back and forth, back and forth, I felt incredibly relaxed. While this was happening, my hands and feet were being gently massaged, making it even more relaxing.

Once the shirodhara was finished, the cloth and cotton balls were removed, I was oiled up, and the body massage began. Sanjay and Manjeet were in perfect sync as their hands slipped up and down the sides of my limp body. For the most part, the two were silent. I kept my eyes closed, mostly because I was so relaxed but also because I didn't want to witness any possible eye communication between the two of them. But then Manjeet whispered something in Hindi that caused me to open my eyes ever so slightly. They were both looking at something and nodding.

When Sanjay noticed that my eyes were open, he smiled broadly and leaned in closer to my face. At first, he said something that I didn't understand, but then he repeated it. It sounded like, "It's so pink!"

I was confused, so I made him repeat it four or five times just to be sure. *Maybe he's saying, "It's so big!"* I thought, *especially since I just spent all that time in the hot sauna. Of course, after steaming for twelve minutes, I am pretty pink, so it could be either.*

At the end of the massage, as they helped me off the table, I almost slid right out of the room. I was literally covered from head to foot in thick Ayurvedic oil. Sanjay came to the rescue and pushed me to the locker room. I didn't even have to lift my feet as he glided me into the shower area. I quickly showered, dried off, and put on my clothes. As I was exiting the locker room, I suddenly remembered that I had to grab my dignity on the way out.

Totally smitten with the Indian culture, I continued to fly the trip for the next six years. Although it could be challenging at times, there was a magical quality about actually being there. The challenges were almost always on the flights, not the layovers. For a few of those years, I worked as purser or head flight attendant. It was a glorified position, mostly in title only. Basically, I worked in first class while overseeing the other cabins and doing way too much paperwork. And on occasion, I ended up babysitting select flight attendants.

The sheer length of the flight could be absolutely brutal, so sometimes there were meltdowns on the return trip to Chicago. And they were never passenger meltdowns. Most of my colleagues did an outstanding job, working hard to ensure that the passengers were well taken care of. However, there were a handful who only worked hard at getting on my last nerve. They seemed to relish starting as many fires as they could. And, as purser, I found myself busy trying to put out those fires.

The top fire starter was a flight attendant who hailed from Alabama. Let's call her Monique Beaufort. Over the years it had become apparent that, even if her family was of French descent—as she and her surname implied—she had never taken a French course. Or one in English, for that matter. Her trademark introduction, spoken in her heavy southern accent, was, "Hi, y'all. I'm Muneek Byoofort." And then after a well-rehearsed pause, "It's French!"

Monique spent half her time stirring things up and the other half explaining why none of it was her fault. On one particular flight, I went to the back of the airplane to see how my coworkers were doing. It was eerily quiet as the majority of passengers were sleeping.

Water and juice stations had been set up on either side of the galley, and just as I entered, a very well-dressed woman was picking up a large Evian bottle to fill her own smaller bottle. Typically, we would've discouraged this in a polite way, especially if the lips of the bottles touched. But there are exceptions, and since she was painstakingly and carefully pouring with a good six inches between bottles, I didn't feel the need to say anything. However, Monique felt differently. She'd been watching the lady but had waited until she was in full pour before screaming at the top of her lungs, "STOP! THAT IS UNSANITARY AND DISGUSTING! YOU'RE NOT THE ONLY ONE DRINKING OUT OF THAT BOTTLE!"

The poor woman poured the remainder of the bottle all over herself and the floor. Then just as quickly as Monique had berated her, she smiled (insincerely) and approached the still-shaking woman, put her arm around her shoulder, and said, "Now listen, hon, let me explain why I had to yell at ya."

I needed a halon extinguisher to put out that fire.

During the boarding process of another flight, I was in the economy cabin dealing with a minor seating snafu. Monique was on the other side of a nearby partition and didn't know I was there. Passengers on those flights always seemed to have a lot of carry-on luggage, and we were constantly asked to lift the heavy bags into the overhead compartments. But to save ourselves from possible injury, our unspoken mantra was, "You pack it, you lift it."

Monique had several of her own mantras, though. And unfortunately, they were not unspoken. Not knowing I was spying on her, I watched as several people made their way down the aisle. One was a very attractive Indian lady. She was quite stylish in her Western attire and was pulling a Tumi bag behind her. From my estimation, the bag was the exact size recommended for overhead storage, but it apparently wasn't in Monique's eyes.

As the lady lifted it over her head, Monique shrieked, "STOP! DON'T PUT THAT UP THERE! YOU DON'T OWN THAT OVERHEAD BIN! PUT IT UNDER YOUR SEAT!" Humiliated, the poor lady almost dropped the bag on her head. I quickly pushed past Monique and lifted the bag into the overhead compartment, telling the lady it was perfectly fine up there. Monique rushed up the aisle, frantically whispering, "That wasn't my fault! You should've seen the nasty look she gave me." I just shook my head and walked away.

A few months later, as I was looking at a list of the crew I would be working with on that night's flight, I was relieved to see the names of people I really enjoyed. I figured it would no doubt be a drama-free and fun trip. All that came to a screeching halt, however, when someone called in sick at the last minute and Monique was called in to replace them.

Although I was working in first class, we only had a few passengers in that section, so my coworker and I finished the meal service quickly. Because coach was packed, I went to the back to help. And it was just my luck to be teamed up with Monique on the meal cart.

Passengers in coach had the usual choice of a vegetarian or chicken entrée. I winced as Monique asked the first row, "We got chicken or vegetarian. Whaddaya want?"

A beautiful young Indian lady in a window seat said, "May I have the vegetarian meal, please?"

Monique just glared at her before tossing a chicken entrée onto her tray.

The lady saw it and politely said, "I'm so sorry, but I asked for the vegetarian."

Monique snatched it up and literally slammed down a vegetarian entrée in front of the woman. Then she leaned over the cart and, with absolute hatred in her voice, hissed, "I hate them! I hate them all!"

Once we finished and were putting things away in the back galley, I told Monique that I felt her behavior was not only unnecessary and inappropriate but extremely rude. I wanted so much to say more, but I still had to work the return trip with her.

She retorted, "Oh, she didn't hear me! And so what if she did. I believe in bein' honest."

A few hours later, I was in the back again when the attractive Indian lady approached me and asked for a glass of water. As I gave it to her, I started a conversation in hopes of softening the earlier incident. After we talked for a while, she looked at my name tag and said, "You've been very kind, Jim, but I must tell you that because of what I heard from your colleague earlier, I will never fly your airline again." I apologized and told her that I understood. Then she said, "I'd like to file a complaint, but your colleague doesn't even have a name tag on."

Of course, she doesn't, I thought.

"What?" I asked, feigning my surprise. "Monique doesn't have her required name tag on? I'll be sure to have a talk with *Monique* about this!"

The young lady smiled and thanked me.

About two hours before landing, a passenger seated in business class became gravely ill and passed out. When I paged for a doctor, several responded. Among them was the lovely, compassionate, and kind Indian lady sitting in the first row of coach who'd been so wrongly treated by a very unhappy, jealous, and bitter person who never did *anything* wrong.

One of my favorite things about flying to India was the food—not only at the hotel restaurant but also on the airplane. Now, three words you'll *rarely* see together are *best*, *airplane*, and *food*, but the food really was good. It also helped that I had become friends with Ravi, one of the catering representatives. Ravi would bring us leftover food from Air India and Emirates flights, so on the way home, we'd gorge ourselves with tandoori chicken, biryani, aloo gobi, dal, palak paneer, and naan.

One night, Ravi brought us enough food to feed a small Indian village, so, to be polite, we ate every morsel. The next morning, we arrived in Chicago on schedule at 5:00 a.m. I had a Global Entry card, so I was able to clear customs quickly and catch my six o'clock bus to South Bend. Given that I was extremely tired that day, I hoped to take a good nap on the three-hour ride home.

When I boarded the bus, I was surprised to see that it was almost full. Typically, there were only a handful of other passengers on this early morning run. I spotted three of my colleagues who'd just returned from Beijing, so I sat near them. We settled back and began sharing stories about our trips. Suddenly, I felt a funny gurgling in my gut. I tried ignoring it, but it refused to be ignored. It got louder and more urgent. I broke into a cold sweat, wondering why the bus had to be full. There was no way I was going to use that tiny bathroom with people sitting so close to it. The door was nothing more than a thick sheet of cardboard.

The bus made three stops en route to South Bend, with the first one being about an hour from O'Hare. As we headed down I-294 toward Indiana, the rumbling, cramping, and urgency intensified. One of my colleagues said I looked pale and asked if I felt alright. I lied and assured her that I was fine, but inside I was praying I didn't have an accident.

Finally, after what seemed like hours, we arrived at the first stop. Miraculously, every single person besides me got off the bus. There was a lot of luggage to unload, so while the driver was doing that, I bolted to the tiny bathroom and exploded like Mount Vesuvius. After several eruptions, I returned to my seat, relieved and ecstatic to have survived a case of Delhi Belly.

The bus driver, a boisterous Black woman I knew well from my frequent rides, boarded the bus after unloading the last of the luggage. She walked toward me and said, "Looks like it's just you and me, babe!" Then, much to my horror, she proceeded to the back to make sure there were no stowaways in the nasty bathroom.

As soon as I heard the cardboard door open, she bellowed, "WHEW-WEE! OH MY GOD! OOOH! OH LORDY! WHOA! WHAT THE HELL?" I turned slightly, just in time to see her next to the bathroom with her arms flailing. This continued for a few more flails and *Oh my Gods* before she ran up the aisle toward me, wide-eyed, as she hollered, "Holy Jesus, it's following me!"

I was dying a thousand deaths at that moment, knowing this would probably go down as my all-time most embarrassing moment. Then she looked me straight in the eye and asked, "Why? *WWWHHHYYY?*"

I was ready to respond, "Because I had to go!" But before I could, she cut me off.

"*Why* do they do that? Why do they do that on my bus, then they get off and leave us here to suffer with it?"

I closed my mouth, no longer feeling the need to fess up to anything. "I don't know," I replied, shaking my head as I sat back in my seat, hoping to still catch a little nap. I smiled and said a silent thank you to the volcano gods, knowing things could've been a whole lot messier. Literally.

Although he'd heard many of my stories before, toward the end of my six-year stint flying to New Delhi, Rich asked me, "What is India *really* like?"

I couldn't find an answer. I knew I had fallen in love with it on my very first trip, but it's truly something that can't be explained; it just has to be experienced. You have to smell, hear, taste, touch, and see the vibrancy, energy, and beauty of the incredible culture that's been around for over forty-five hundred years. And, unlike the Moniques of the world, you need to open your mind and step out of the box to see the beauty of something so wonderfully diverse and different. It's a simple choice of being limited or unlimited. I happily choose unlimited.

Laugh That
One Off

A fter over sixteen years together, Rich and I were chomping at the bit to design and build our dream house. When
we first moved in together in 1982, we lived in a one-bedroom
apartment for a couple years. From there, we bought our first
place, a small Cape Cod that we fixed up and happily remained
in for the next fourteen years. We loved that little house but
always held on to the hope of someday using our creative juices
to design our dream home. During those fourteen years, we also
bought and flipped two small fixer-uppers. We scrimped and
saved over the next few years until the day finally came when we
placed a for sale sign in our front lawn.

Naively assuming it would take several months to sell, we
weren't in a huge hurry to accomplish the usual steps associated
with selling a house—like packing and having a place to live in
the interim while the new place was being built. But we soon
realized that we should never assume because the house sold on
the very first day it was on the market to the first person who

walked in the door. This threw us into a panic because it could take months—possibly even a year—before our new house would be finished.

It wasn't as if we were *totally* unprepared, though. A few months earlier, we had purchased a lot in a small subdivision. But short of pitching a tent there during the building process, we really didn't have an alternate plan.

As is often the case, though, panic is unnecessary if you just step back and let the universe do its magic. After all, we did own a rental house next door, and ironically, the day after our house sold, the tenants informed us that they would be leaving in a month. It worked out perfectly. The sale of our current home was closing in thirty days, so we simply moved our belongings next door during the last week of May.

But as the plans for the new place escalated, so did the price tag. Even so, we knew this would be our one and only "dream house," so we wanted to do it right. The builder was extremely busy that summer, so he proposed breaking ground at the end of August. That gave us three more months to become increasingly nervous about the quickly rising cost. So we decided to put the rental house on the market at the beginning of August. Obviously, we had not learned our lesson because we again assumed it would take a while to sell. But just like our other house, it sold to the first person who looked at it.

At this point, we started having colitis attacks as we stressed over where we'd live for the next few months. But then my sweet little mother made us a generous offer. "You can come stay with me." By *you*, she was referring to her older son (me), his homosexual partner, and their furry canine son, Reggie, a rambunctious, yet loving, terrier mix.

We moved in with Mom at the end of August. Later, I over-heard her telling a friend, "When they were moving their stuff in—and they had *a lot* of stuff—I got a little nervous when I saw Christmas wrapping paper! I thought they'd be moved out by then." But even though there were some challenging moments, we made the best of our seven months under one roof and cre-ated some fun memories.

Closing on our new house took place in March of 1999. We loved it from the start. It was in a great location and a perfect neighborhood. The thing that we, two OCD gay guys, loved most about our neighborhood was that everyone took such good care of their houses and lawns.

Our lot was near the front of the subdivision, but we knew that the heavily wooded lots between us and the entrance would probably be sold at some point. An elderly lady named Maria lived on the other side of us. When we met her, she told us how glad she was not to be next to the wooded area any-more. Apparently, on a few occasions, young people had used the woods for what young people do—or in Maria's words, "drinking and necking."

Sadly, Maria passed away a few years later, and within a cou-ple months, her house sold. I met the new occupant on closing day as she strolled around the property. We talked over the fence that separated our backyards for what seemed like—and possibly could've been—hours. Let me rephrase that: I listened while *she* talked, divulging her entire life story. I would've preferred the *Reader's Digest* condensed version, but that was not to be. To be fair, it wasn't her *entire* life story, just the first forty-five years or so. It started with, "My parents always told me they wanted a boy."

From there, she shared more than I really wanted to know:

"I just couldn't stand living with my husband anymore."

"My job sucks."

"I gained all this weight because of him."

"My son hates me."

What was interesting and majorly irritating, though, was that after almost every single sentence, she added, "Laugh that one off!"

"I should've gotten that promotion. Laugh that one off!"

"He had no right to give me that speeding ticket! Laugh that one off!"

"My father was so cheap he refused to buy steel toe boots and dropped an anchor on his foot. He got gangrene and ended up losing half of his foot. Laugh that one off!"

"I almost died when I had my hysterectomy. Laugh that one off!"

About halfway through her monologue, I wasn't sure whether I should be laughing or running away.

Instead, I just listened. There was absolutely no way of interrupting her. She droned on and on and on, regaling me with stories of how her soon-to-be ex had turned all their relatives—including her own kids—against her.

"He's such a control freak . . . never even let me finish a sentence. Laugh that one off!"

"Really? He was that—?" I tried.

"And a real womanizer. Even when I was skinny. Do you know how much I used to weigh?"

"How mu—"

"I used to weigh 119 pounds! Laugh that one off!"

"How many childr—"

"My oldest son has even stopped talking to me, just like his father. Laugh that one off!"

"That's terr—"

But then her tone suddenly changed, "The only thing that's kept me going is Butterfingers."

"Oh, you like candy bars?" It was a miracle! I'd actually finished a sentence.

"Huh? No, Butterfingers is my dog."

"Oh, you're an animal lover too?"

"Yes, did I tell you he bit me on Mother's Day? Laugh that one off!"

"Who? Butterfingers?"

"No, my husband! Besides, Butterfingers is a she. He bit me hard too—my husband, that is. Soon-to-be *ex* husband! Laugh that one off!"

"So it's just you and Butterfingers now?"

"And the kitties."

"Oh, how many kitties do you have?"

"Just a couple. And *he* insisted on keeping my favorite one, KitKat! Laugh that one off!"

And on and on it went.

Within a couple of days, it became apparent that our new neighbor's interpretation of "just a couple" was quite different than ours. Something else that quickly became apparent was that she loved candy. Before we knew it, Hershey, Chuckles, Baby Ruth, Tootsie, Jujube, and Chunky were visiting us daily. Now, don't get me wrong, I love all animals, especially dogs and cats. But I'm not crazy about humans who don't take care of their dogs and cats.

Within three months, which happens to be the gestation period of a cat, there were pussies *everywhere*. Why is that?

Because Hershey, Chuckles, Baby Ruth, Tootsie, Jujube, and Chunky were not fixed. Turns out the only pet of hers who had been fixed was Butterfingers.

Before we knew it, we had cats and kittens on the front porch, in the bushes, in the garage, climbing the sides of our screened porch, and basically using our entire lawn, garden, and pool area as one gigantic litter box.

Their human seemed absolutely oblivious, perhaps because they were never at her house. Butterfingers, who was never on a leash, started to come visit us too. Fearing for the little dog's safety, I tried reasoning with our neighbor.

"We live on a very busy street," I began.

"But she's used to living on a quiet cul-de-sac," the neighbor said a little too defensively.

"This is anything *but* a quiet cul-de-sac," I replied.

It went in one ear and out the other. Laugh that one off!

One day, I was dangling from a ten-foot ladder, washing windows. Directly below the ladder was a large ceramic chiminea. Although a chiminea is typically used as an outdoor fireplace, ours had never been home to so much as a glowing ember. Instead, thanks to Rich's creative ability and his recent penchant for watching *Martha Stewart Living*, he'd turned it into an outdoor fashion statement. In the hole at the top of the pear-shaped unit, he'd placed a large pot overflowing with green ivy. Inside the hole of the rounded bottom, he'd sprinkled a bag of sand to weigh it down. The whole thing was balanced on a base with three spindly, yet sturdy, legs.

On this particular day, as I was spit shining the upper windows, Rich was trimming the boxwoods that bordered the patio. With an ever so gentle breeze blowing, from my perch above the chiminea, I kept getting a less than pleasant whiff of something rank. I finally asked Rich if he was farting, and when he assured me that he wasn't, I said, "Did something die in the chiminea?"

Rich obediently walked over to it and stuck his entire head into the large hole in the front. Within seconds, he was convulsing with dry heaves and bonking his head as he tried to get it out of the hole. I, being the kind and understanding soul that I am, almost fell off the ladder because I, too, was convulsing . . . with laughter.

"Those damn cats shit in my chiminea!" he screamed so loud that several felines made hasty exits from their various hiding places. "How in the *hell* many cats does she have now?"

As I climbed down the ladder, I said, "Uh . . . last I counted, there were sixteen."

"*Sixteen?* That's it," he said, lowering his voice as he pushed past me into the house. "I'm calling the city and finding out just how many animals one household is allowed."

Now, it's not that Rich doesn't care for animals. On the contrary, he loves both dogs and cats too. But again, when they're cared for properly. These animals clearly were not being cared for properly. Our new neighbor was obviously consumed by her impending divorce and other dramas that she no doubt had created. But *we* were being consumed by her refusal to be responsible for her pets.

And we weren't the only ones. Over the next few weeks and months—and several litters later—other neighbors started complaining. The neighborhood was being *overrun* with pussies. Something had to be done, and it had to be done quickly. So the homeowner's association contacted a no-kill shelter to trap the majority of them, and a mobile spaying unit was sent to sterilize several of them. New homes were found for Chuckles, Hershey,

Jujube, and Chunky, along with several others, leaving only Butterfingers, Baby Ruth, and Tootsie behind.

Once it was devoid of the incessant screaming and hissing of feral cats and the litter box stench that permeated our outdoor areas, our quiet and pleasant-smelling neighborhood finally returned to normal.

Our next-door neighbor wasn't happy, though. In fact, she stopped speaking to us because she mistakenly assumed we were the ones who had called the authorities. Regardless of who actually called them, it had to be done. Those poor animals had no life. And her not speaking to us was . . . well, not such a bad thing. Laugh that one off!

But Butterfingers—sweet, pudgy, begging for attention Butterfingers—held no grudges whatsoever and continued to visit us often. Her human broke the silent treatment one day, just long enough to inform me in a less than neighborly tone, "Butterfingers doesn't even *like* you! She just wants the treats you're bribing her with."

I didn't even respond because I knew deep down that Butterfingers came to our house for love and attention, not the carrot sticks I offered. She could care less about those. She would go from our front door to our back door, scratching at both, to let us know she was there for a visit. Once she was inside, she'd spend many contented hours snuggling on our laps.

One evening, while we were sitting on our patio, Rich mouthed to me, "She's headed this way." I looked at him with confusion, wondering who he was referring to.

"How are you guys doing?"

I turned around and the neighbor was standing there. Apparently, she'd forgotten that she hadn't spoken to us in years. But there she was, acting as though we were best friends, just chatting and catching up. And she had *a lot* of catching up to do.

"They had no right to fire me! Laugh that one off!"

"I think someone broke into my house and stole things out of my refrigerator! Laugh that one off!"

"I know I paid that water bill! I have half a mind to sue because I was without water for a week! Laugh that one off!"

"The roofers tried to rip me off when they put on my new roof. So I threatened to have them deported. They disappeared so fast, I never even paid them. Laugh that one off!"

"My daughter is getting married and doesn't want me at the wedding! Can you believe that? Me, her own mother! Laugh that one off!"

As Rich's eyes met mine, we were obviously thinking the same thing: *How can we piss her off enough to return to our nice peaceful existence?*

"So did you ever find out who turned you in for animal abuse?" I asked, trying to sound as innocent as possible.

She glared at me.

"How's the divorce going? Is it finalized yet?"

If looks could kill . . .

"I love our neighborhood. I just wish everyone took care of their property."

Voilà! She turned and stomped off, leaving us once again in total peace, solitude, and silence.

Laugh that one off!

PITA

It's often said that God will never give us more than we can handle, which makes me strongly suspect that he or she has never had butt surgery. Otherwise, I'm sure he or she used his or her own powers to heal quickly and painlessly. Unfortunately, I don't possess those powers, so my own healing was neither quick nor painless when I had it done. Far from it.

I really didn't just wake up one morning and think, *Boy, I sure hope I can have butt surgery!* True, I had been the recipient of several hemorrhoids over the years, but thus far, diet modification, laxatives, and creams had been effective in treating them. But then those home remedies stopped working, and the little buggers started becoming more bothersome and painful. After arriving home from a particularly long and grueling flight with a rear end that looked like I was blowing a bubble out of it, I knew it was time for drastic measures. So I called my primary physician, who had been recommending surgery for some time. He got me in quickly and while examining the affected area, he said, "Jesus, Jim! How are you even walking with that thing?" At that point, he referred me to a butt doctor. I believe the actual title is colorectal doctor, but "butt doctor" rolls off the tongue much more easily.

I liked Dr. Dellanova from the minute he opened the door . . . so to speak. He was an affable guy with a quick wit, which is admirable for someone who literally deals with assholes. He did a thorough exam, much to my embarrassment, and determined right away that surgery was necessary. He explained the entire procedure, how long it would take, and the recuperation process before adding, "And it's going to hurt like hell!" Total honesty was obviously another one of his endearing traits.

Despite my knowledge of the forthcoming pain, Butt Surgery Day, or as I called it BSD, could not arrive soon enough. In preparation, I made a trip to the pharmacy the day before. Since I'd never had anything of this nature done, I tried to imagine what might be useful during my recuperation. As I walked up and down the aisles, scouring the shelves, I spotted the inflatable doughnuts. I tossed one in my cart before noticing the adult diapers next to them. As I looked over all the different types available, I was a bit surprised to see one with a special pouch in the front that was designed specifically for the male anatomy. *That could be very useful*, I thought, so I grabbed a package and put it between the doughnut and the sitz bath I had already found. Then I spotted the Epsom salt and some "soothing" bubble bath. *Boy, am I going to have a happy bum!*

The next morning, Rich and I arrived at the hospital at six. After I disrobed and put on a flimsy hospital gown, I was prepped and was soon IV-ready. The anesthesiologist entered my cubicle and explained what anesthesia he would be administering. As he left, Dr. Dellanova came in and greeted us. He again went over what he would be doing, then asked if I had any questions.

"Just one," I said. "Do you wear a face shield during surgery?"

He laughed and asked, "No, should I?"

I told him that although I had followed the prep procedure instructions to a tee, I still didn't feel quite "emptied out."

He told me not to worry and assured me that they were prepared for anything. As he was walking out and looking over my chart one last time, he said, "Well, would you look at that? We're neighbors!"

I asked if he lived in our small subdivision.

"No, but I'm right around the corner on Sycamore. It's the house that sits way back from the road."

Those were the last words I heard and registered before the anesthesia sent me to an incredibly euphoric place.

I was still numb when we left the hospital a few hours later. On the way home, Rich kept worriedly asking how I was.

"Never been better. I just *love* the drugs they used," I slurred.

"No, I mean, how's your butt? Are you in pain?"

I wasn't. On the contrary, I had no feeling whatsoever down there.

When we arrived home, Rich insisted on helping me get out of the car. Then he took my arm and helped me ascend the three stairs from the garage to the house. Once inside, he helped me get undressed, blew up my doughnut, and filled a large bag with ice. I put the ice pack in the front pouch of my new male diaper. I'd chosen size XL to allow more room for my ice bag. Once that was done, per my instructions, Rich helped me put the diaper on backward. Finally, he helped me squeeze into my new, black

XXL sweatpants. I looked like a butt-implanted Kardashian with absolutely no fashion sense.

I waddled out of the bathroom with Rich shouting from behind, "You really need to get on your doughnut!"

I went into the den and stood in front of the window, mindlessly thinking, "Well, that whole thing wasn't so bad." Then, all of a sudden, I felt a sensation—or rather an urge—not unlike I typically do after my first sip of coffee in the morning. It was extremely mild at first but soon became more urgent. I remembered the colonoscopies I'd endured in the past and how I was always instructed to expel all the trapped gas—of which there seemed to be an endless supply. So I expelled. Boy, did I expel!

Worried as to what I was going to find in the back of my diaper, which was technically the front, I quietly shuffled to the bathroom. But I really didn't find what I thought I would find. Instead, there was a large wad of bloody gauze, which, when unraveled, was about thirty-five feet long. I cleaned up and changed my own diaper before waddling back to the den to read the discharge orders.

"DO NOT REMOVE PACKING FOR 24 HOURS" was the first thing I saw. *Uh-oh.* Mine had only spent three, maybe four, hours in its cozy resting spot. I was worried that I'd have to have more crammed up there, so I immediately called the butt doctor's office. I closed the door to the den to prevent Rich from hearing, then in a hushed whisper, I babbled on and on about how I didn't realize it would come out from what was supposed to be just one simple toot. The kind lady assured me that it was fine. I wouldn't have to be repacked.

A little after seven that evening, twelve hours after my surgery and right in the middle of *Wheel of Fortune*, all things anesthesia-related wore off. It wasn't a gradual process either. I was numb one second and in excruciating pain the next. At that point in my life, I'd experienced pain a few times. The two hernia surgeries I'd endured were not what I considered fun any more than when I had my tonsils yanked out when I was twenty-one. The tonsil part wasn't so bad, but when my uvula was accidentally whacked off in the process, it was no walk in the park. Then there was the time I walked around on a broken foot for five days. Add twelve kidney stones and all the accidents and subsequent stitches I've had over the years and, well, I'm not exactly a stranger to major suffering. But I usually try to do it quietly. I'm pretty sure I was blessed with my mother's high tolerance for pain. This time was different, though—in the most agonizing, excruciating, searing, intense, racking, violent way I'd ever known.

That night, to ensure my uncontrollable moaning and pacing (or, more specifically, shuffling back and forth, back and forth, back and forth because I didn't want to sit or lie down) didn't keep Rich awake, I moved to the spare bedroom. The next morning after no sleep whatsoever, I made my way to the kitchen. Rich was extremely concerned, so I gave a stellar performance to make him think I felt better. At one point, I opened the back door.

"*What* are you doing, Jim?" he asked, surprised that I was even up and moving.

"I'm going to get the newspaper."

He looked concerned and eyed me before saying, "Well, . . . be careful!"

As I started down our long driveway, which up until that point hadn't seemed long at all, I wondered how I could make it all the way to the mailbox. As I concentrated on one painful step after another, I didn't even notice two ladies walking a dog until we all reached the mailbox at the same time. Even with my intense discomfort, I felt a bit embarrassed about how I looked.

One of the ladies greeted me and said, "We just love your landscaping!"

I thanked her and added, "I'll be sure to tell the person who's responsible," which was Rich, not me.

We all introduced ourselves and continued talking. Linda was the mother of the younger lady, Tina, and Jake was Tina's beagle child. I had seen them walking through the neighborhood many times before. We talked about landscaping, the weather, Jake, and pretty much everything else except why I had such a big lumpy ass. When I asked if they lived in the subdivision, Linda responded, "No, we're right around the corner on Sycamore. It's the house that sits way back from the road."

I knew I'd heard that same thing recently and racked my brain trying to remember where. When it suddenly hit me, I asked, "Is your husband a doctor?"

She looked at me, surprised, and answered, "He is! How did you know?"

"Talk about a small world," I said. "He did my surgery yesterday!"

Linda looked really surprised—bewildered, actually. She looked at me for a moment, then shook her head and said, "I just can't believe you had back surgery yesterday, and you're home and walking today!"

I returned her stare as the wheels of my now somewhat-clear brain turned, and the light bulb suddenly went on. "My surgery was . . . uh . . . *lower.*"

I waited for her light bulb to go on, and it did, much quicker than mine had. "Oh!" she laughed. "That's our next-door neighbor, Tim Dellanova!"

We talked a while longer before saying goodbye. I laboriously and painfully made my way back up the driveway, which seemed longer and steeper than I'd ever noticed before.

"Where *were* you? I was getting worried!" Rich was on me the minute I walked in the house. Not worried enough to look out the window to see if I was lying in a pool of blood or anything, but worried nonetheless.

"I was talking to some people walking by."

"For *forty-five* minutes?" he asked incredulously.

As I recounted the whole story, he looked mortified in the way only Rich can look mortified when I tell him a story. "You told *perfect strangers* you just had butt surgery?" he asked in total disbelief.

"No!" I said. "I told my new friends Linda, Tina, and Jake I just had butt surgery. They're not strangers!"

Later that day, I mentioned that I needed to go see my mom. We had just moved her into a new condo the day before my surgery, and I wanted to make sure she and her Yorkie, Teddy, were doing okay.

"You can't drive!" Rich informed me, which is exactly what I wanted to hear. He stared at me for a moment, then said, "I'll take you."

When we arrived, Mom met us at the door with Teddy by her feet. He was excitedly bouncing around, happy to see us, when something suddenly caught his attention, and he bolted out the door of his new home and headed toward a very busy street. Forgetting what I had just experienced the day before, I took off after him. Call it adrenaline or call it divine butt intervention, but I think I did a hundred meters in twelve seconds. Teddy was still ahead of me, but when he saw a golden retriever in a nearby yard, he stopped dead in his tracks to attempt to smell the larger dog's hind end. Teddy—all nine pounds of him—was on his back haunches, stretched to the max, trying desperately to get a good whiff. I grabbed him mid-sniff.

It was only then, as I started waddling back to my mom's place with Teddy wiggling to get out of my arms so he could tend to something much more aromatic, that I realized I probably shouldn't have gone for a run the day after surgery.

For the next several days, I tried to be sensible and somewhat immobile. The only comfort I could get, although minuscule, was sitting in the bathtub. I spent so much time in the tub that I soon looked like a waterlogged and withered raisin. Each time I lowered myself into the water, I couldn't help but let out a very loud moan, similar to the ones on cartoons when someone's keister is on fire and they suddenly find a bucket of water to sit in.

Other than shooting the packing out and my hundred-meter sprint, I followed all the instructions verbatim, right down to the stool softeners. Finally, several days later, the pain was almost tolerable. When I returned to Dr. Dellanova's office for a follow-up visit, he seemed happy with both my progress and his sewing job. He explained that once he got "up there," he was surprised to find several more pesky hemorrhoids in addition to a fissure *and* a fistula, whatever those were.

"I found everything except Jimmy Hoffa up there!" he joked.

But my laughter was short-lived because it still hurt. It wasn't quite as bad as when I hacked, coughed, sneezed, or farted, but it still hurt.

Several years later, sporting my still somewhat new bunghole, I was at the hospital with my mother, who was having minor out-patient surgery. While sitting in the waiting room, one of the doors opened and Dr. Dellanova walked through. He was wear-ing scrubs, and he seemed to be in a hurry as he scurried past me. But when our eyes met, he stopped, backed up, and said, "Well, hello there! How are you doing? It's been what . . . three or four years now?"

I was impressed not only with his good memory but that he even recognized me. "You remember my *face*?"

"Yes, on occasion I even look at faces!" he chuckled.

I thanked Dr. Dellanova right then and there and told him he was a true artist in his field. His face reddened ever so slightly, even though I'm pretty sure he was very proud of his work. It was a masterpiece of sorts, one that could be titled, *Where the Sun Don't Shine*.

Epilogue

When I was seven, I used my weekly allowance to buy a little diary from the local five-and-dime store. Typically, these were popular with little girls, but even then, I was anything but typical. It soon became my best friend and confidant as I shared my deepest thoughts, dreams, hopes, desires, and fantasies. I could—and did—tell it everything.

I continued journaling through college. While backpacking through Europe for four months when I was twenty, I was often very lonely. But I always found comfort knowing my journal was right there, waiting for me to put all my thoughts and secrets into written words. During those four months of traveling, I wrote and wrote and wrote—four "volumes" to be exact. Recently, I reread them and suddenly knew why they had been so beneficial to me at the time. They contained every detail of a very defining period of exploration and self-discovery for me, something I was too terrified to discuss with any other person. But my journals never judged, never criticized, never ridiculed, and never laughed at me when I shared anything and everything. They simply listened. And it felt good to be heard.

Writing can be so therapeutic and healing, and I now realize that's the biggest reason I do it. And I will continue to do it because I still have a *lot* to analyze and try to figure out in this never-ending therapy session called life.

Stay tuned . . .

Acknowledgments

To my father and late mother, Ed and Barbara, thank you for always inspiring me to do the very best I could. Your unwavering love and support gave me the courage and motivation to work hard and make my dreams come true. Our journey was not always easy. I watched and learned from you as you lost your own parents, siblings, friends, and grandson. The biggest fear I ever had was that I would someday lose my mother. And when that day actually came, instead of fear, my heart was overflowing with intense gratitude for having been a part of each other's lives in the first place. Even in death, you, my precious mom, continue to embrace and teach me. The love and memories will live on forever.

To my siblings, Deb and Scott, although there was nothing ordinary or traditional about our upbringing, we were always well taken care of, well loved, and we always had fun. I'm so blessed to have shared those years with you. Thank you for always being there for me.

And to all my dear friends, which I've been blessed with many: even though we may go several years without seeing one another, the love and unbreakable bond we share is always present. Each of you has been there—at one time or another—to pick me up, listen to me, laugh with me, get into trouble with me, or simply be with me. I'm so grateful that you're in my life.

Thank you to my incredible editor, Jennifer Huston Schaeffer of White Dog Editorial Services. Your patience, knowledge, dedication, guidance, and editing magic are so appreciated. Your gentle words of encouragement have always come at exactly the right time for me, and I'm really looking forward to working with you on future projects.

To my book designer, Domini Dragoone. You're a wellspring of creativity, and your work is amazing. Thank you for bringing it all together so perfectly.

To all my LGBTQIA+ brothers and sisters, your commitment and perseverance to live and love in your own diverse uniqueness is such an inspiration. What a beautiful kaleidoscope we have all created together. Each of us is absolutely perfect in God's eyes, *just the way we are.*

And last but not least, to the love of my life, Rich: I can't imagine life without you. You have stood by my side every step of the way, even when I haven't been the kindest or most lovable soul. Patience is one of your greatest virtues, and I saw that from the very beginning. I love spending time with you, whether we're on some fun-filled adventure or simply sitting next to each other in total silence. We've grown so much together over the past four decades, and I look forward to many more years of living, loving, and laughing as only we can.

About the Author

J ames Pauley, Jr. was born and raised in a small town in southwestern Michigan. He received his bachelor's degree from Albion College, with a double major in German and Spanish. Spending a semester each in Guadalajara, Mexico, and Heidelberg, Germany, piqued his interest and lifelong love of international travel. He began his career as a flight attendant in 1978, a job that he continues to enjoy. Throughout his life, he's worn many other hats as well: massage therapist, real estate agent, house flipper, painter, busboy, groundskeeper, delivery person, wine steward, waiter, babysitter, caterer, house cleaner, bartender, cake decorator, window washer, substitute teacher, janitor, and salesman. He is the coauthor of *Granny and the Gay Guy* with best-selling author Charlene Potterbaum. He lives with his spouse, Rich, in Indiana.

You can connect with
Jim via the following:

www.jpauleyauthor.com

Twitter: @JamesPauley23

Instagram: @jpauley23

Facebook: @jamespauleyauthor

Made in USA - Kendallville, IN
66618_9798986751610
08.10.2023 1357